To Suffolk With Love

The life of
Felix Thornley Cobbold

Rosalind Thomas

Copyright © 2009 Cobbold Family History Trust

ISBN 978-0-9548298-9-6

Edited by Pip Wright
Published by **Pawprint Publishing**
14, Polstead Close, Stowmarket, Suffolk   IP14 2PJ

1st reprint September 2012

To Suffolk with love

The life of
Felix Thornley Cobbold
1841 - 1909

Felix
Thornley
Cobbold

Contents

COBBOLD FAMILY TREE

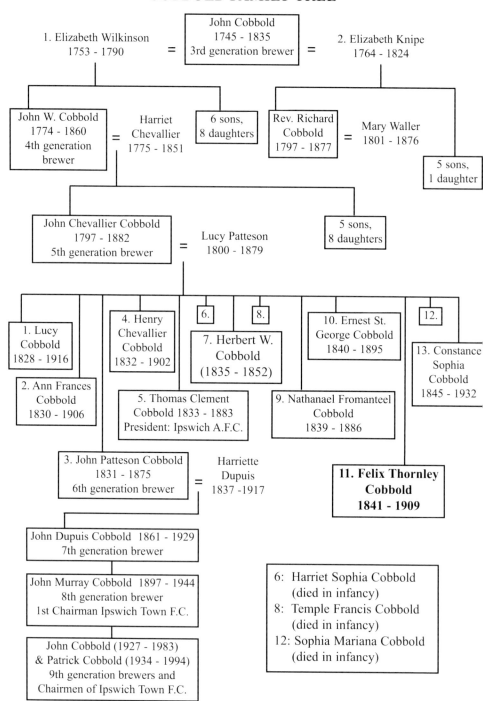

1. Elizabeth Wilkinson
1753 - 1790

=

John Cobbold
1745 - 1835
3rd generation brewer

=

2. Elizabeth Knipe
1764 - 1824

John W. Cobbold
1774 - 1860
4th generation
brewer

=

Harriet
Chevallier
1775 - 1851

6 sons,
8 daughters

Rev. Richard
Cobbold
1797 - 1877

=

Mary Waller
1801 - 1876

5 sons,
1 daughter

John Chevallier Cobbold
1797 - 1882
5th generation brewer

=

Lucy Patteson
1800 - 1879

5 sons,
8 daughters

1. Lucy
Cobbold
1828 - 1916

2. Ann Frances
Cobbold
1830 - 1906

4. Henry
Chevallier
Cobbold
1832 - 1902

5. Thomas Clement
Cobbold 1833 - 1883
President: Ipswich A.F.C.

6.

7. Herbert W.
Cobbold
(1835 - 1852)

8.

10. Ernest St.
George Cobbold
1840 - 1895

9. Nathanael Fromanteel
Cobbold
1839 - 1886

12.

13. Constance
Sophia
Cobbold
1845 - 1932

3. John Patteson Cobbold
1831 - 1875
6th generation brewer

=

Harriette
Dupuis
1837 -1917

**11. Felix Thornley
Cobbold
1841 - 1909**

John Dupuis Cobbold 1861 - 1929
7th generation brewer

John Murray Cobbold 1897 - 1944
8th generation brewer
1st Chairman Ipswich Town F.C.

John Cobbold (1927 - 1983)
& Patrick Cobbold (1934 - 1994)
9th generation brewers and
Chairmen of Ipswich Town F.C.

6: Harriet Sophia Cobbold
(died in infancy)
8: Temple Francis Cobbold
(died in infancy)
12: Sophia Mariana Cobbold
(died in infancy)

6

Introduction

I began this book seventeen years ago while working for Otley College in mid Suffolk. The Felix Thornley Cobbold Trust was our landlord, and generous in helping us with additional funding. I decided to find out more about the man who had endowed the Trust, and initially visited the late Patrick Cobbold at Glemham Hall. Patrick helped me with information about the family and the brewery, and also lent me a wonderful leather-bound volume of obituaries compiled, I think, by Felix's sister, Constance.

As I began to read the obituaries I developed an admiration for Felix Cobbold. He was intelligent, cultured, humorous, a good financier and a banker with a human touch. His radical political views were always coloured by his real sympathy for the clients who came to him struggling with the adverse trade conditions: the small farmers facing ruin after a bad season, the labourers who came to listen to him speak, and who took their right to vote almost as a religious duty, the armed forces facing danger in a pointless war, the bright young man needing a patron to enable him to go to university - all engaged his interest and created a feeling that it was his duty to help in any way he could.

Above all, it was the plight of the agricultural labourers that touched him most. Inspired by the ideas of Jesse Collings and Joseph Chamberlain, he devoted the rest of his life to creating wealth which would be channelled into providing smallholdings and allotments and thereby enabling destitute labourers to return to the land and earn a living wage to support their families.

During the last few years I have studied both with Dr Frank Grace via the University of East Anglia adult education classes, and then with the staff of the History Department at the University of Essex on a Masters' course. This work enlarged my knowledge of agricultural history, and the political scene in nineteenth century Suffolk to enable me to put Felix in context. The book has now been completed to coincide with the centenary of the death of Felix Cobbold and the intended exhibition at Christchurch Mansion.

I would also like to thank and acknowledge the help given me by the Suffolk Record Office, the Albert Sloman Library, University of Essex, the Lloyds Bank Archivist, and the Archivist at King's College, Cambridge. I have also been helped by Anthony Cobbold of the Cobbold Family History Trust and other members of the Cobbold family. In addition, the managers of the Felix Thornley Cobbold Agricultural Trust (now renamed Felix Cobbold Trust) both in the 1990s and this year have given me information about the Trust and the recent changes to its form and purpose.

Rosalind Thomas
Colchester, 2009

Illustrations

We would like to thank the following for permission to reproduce illustrations:
Birmingham Libraries and Archives: page 20
David Kindred: pages 10, 36, 42, 45, 46, 47, 48, 49
Des Codd: page 25
Cobbold Family History Trust: pages 29, 30, 31, 32, 33
Felix Cobbold Trust: page 78
Colchester & Ipswich Museums: Collier portrait, cover and page 50
Leonard R. Squirrell's executors: page 40
Lloyds TSB Group Archives: page 38, Ref A/53/63/1/4
Otley College: page 77
Suffolk Record Office, Ipswich Branch: page 32

Chapter 1: Felix Thornley Cobbold (1841-1909)

Felix Thornley Cobbold was a nineteenth century philanthropist, the son of John Chevallier Cobbold and Lucy Patteson, whose gifts to the community are still benefitting Ipswich, and the agricultural industry of East Anglia, but who is today largely unknown to the public at large. 2009 is the centenary of his death, so this book was written to record the work of this remarkable man.

To understand the man we must first look at his family: he was born at Holy Wells Mansion[1] in Ipswich, John Chevallier's seventh son and ninth child, part of a large and wealthy family devoted to public service. They were energetic, intelligent, and good at both producing and managing money.

The Cobbold brewery

Most people in Suffolk will immediately identify the Cobbolds as brewers, but their wider influence on the town means that in Ipswich and also in Felixstowe there are streets named after various members of the family, such as Chevallier Street, and the site of the family mansion at Holy Wells still contains some of the outbuildings and the famous springs themselves, enclosed in a public park.

The Cobbolds trace their family from Robert Cobbold, a yeoman of Tostock, who died in 1603, but the family business was begun by Thomas Cobbold in 1723 in Harwich. He had previously been a maltster, and he realised that there was an opportunity for a brewing enterprise supplying beer to the troops at Landguard fort, opposite Harwich, and also to the warships calling at the port for revictualling. However, there were a number of other breweries already in existence, and wine importing had been an important part of local trade since the thirteenth century. Thomas realized that his business must set new standards for production methods and efficiency if it was to produce a beer of consistently high quality. He and his son, another Thomas, travelled widely to inspect and purchase the most up-to-date equipment. He chose so well that one of the original coppers was still used for priming in the Ipswich brewery in the 1970s.

---

[1] Felix referred to his family home as Holy Wells rather than the more usual Holywells, and I have used this spelling throughout the book.

His biggest success, however, was to realise that the water supply was crucial to the quality of the product, and so rejected the brackish Harwich water in favour of water brought from the clear springs of the family estate at Holy Wells. For twenty-three years he continued to bring tubs of water down the Orwell by ship, which returned full of beer casks. However, in 1746 he made the decision to take the brewery to the water instead of the water to the brewery, and built his new premises on the Cliff site in Ipswich, where it remains to this day. The eldest son in each generation always became head of the brewery, since, whatever other business interests the family were involved in, the brewery continued to be the heart of their wealth and standing in the community

The mansion at Holy Wells in 1905.

The family further developed their shipping interests after moving the brewery and by 1850 owned more than twenty ships, which traded as far as India and China, and, typically, many were named after members of the family. For example, a ship built in 1865 was named "Constance", who was a sister of Felix Cobbold.

The Cobbolds and Ipswich

Ipswich in the nineteenth century was prosperous and expanding. Traditionally the landowners of the country returned Tory members to Parliament, but during the century there were a number of measures to reform suffrage and local government that had a profound influence on the area. In 1832 Parliament passed the Great Reform Bill which gave the vote to men in boroughs occupying houses with an annual value of £10. Although an improvement, this meant that only one in seven men could vote, and pressure remained for further changes. In 1835 the Municipal Reform Act allowed 178 boroughs, including Ipswich, to form their own town councils, with all rate payers eligible to vote in council elections. The towns were divided into wards which each contributed councillors, and they in turn could elect a Mayor and aldermen. The new councils gradually took over responsibility for local affairs such as the police force, housing, education, water supplies etc. and thus controlled much of the governance of the boroughs.

The Cobbold family decided to take an active part in the new administration. John Cobbold (1774-1860) contested St Clement's ward in 1835 (which included the brewery and the Holy Wells estate) as a Tory, but was defeated, as was his eldest son, John Chevallier, in the Westgate ward. The following year, however, the Corporation of Ipswich was formed, with a mayor, aldermen, and councillors, and John senior was elected to St Clement's ward. He continued to hold the ward until 1855 almost continuously (being defeated by one vote in 1840), and was made an alderman in 1847.

In 1825 he joined the board of the Ipswich Town & Country bank, and it was the family's wealth and good name that helped the bank to survive at a time when banks all over the country were collapsing. Later, his son John Chevallier also joined the board.

John Chevallier Cobbold (1797-1882)

John Chevallier Cobbold was elected to the Westgate ward in 1838-41, also as a Tory, and was elected Mayor of Ipswich in 1841. He was clearly a man of strong character who had a profound effect on young Felix. He had been educated at Bury St Edmunds Grammar

11

School. He qualified as a solicitor and had a law office in Tower Street, Ipswich, and then in 1827 he married Lucy Patteson, the daughter of Reverend H. Patteson, rector of Drinkstone and sister of Sir John Patteson, QC. The marriage was long and happy, and their Golden Wedding celebrations at Holy Wells on May 14 1877 were recorded in great detail in the press. John survived his wife by five years, finally succumbing to a chill caught while out driving.

He had wide business interests. Apart from his law firm, as eldest son he inherited the brewery from his father in 1860, and remained on the board of the bank. He was one of the founders of the new Anglesea Road Hospital Board and continued as its Treasurer until his death. He also owned a small farm close to the family cottage at Cobbold Point, Felixstowe.

Typically, he also became involved in the affairs of Felixstowe Town as well as Ipswich, becoming a trustee of the Poor's Estate, and a substantial landowner in the area. Several charming villas still exist near the Spa which he had built to serve the needs of the growing population of the town on land which he had bought from the Duke of Hamilton. In 1839 he also built the Bath Hotel, (originally called the Hamilton Arms) using stone taken from the demolished Martello Tower.

He became chairman of the Eastern Union Railway Company until it was absorbed by the Eastern Counties Railway Company, and in 1844 secured the necessary legislation in Parliament to connect Ipswich with the existing railway line at Colchester. Simultaneously he constructed a line connecting Ipswich with Bury St Edmunds. This line opened in 1846, and three years later was extended to Norwich. The whole area prospered with this improvement in communications, and the Ipswich population increased by nearly 50% as local manufacturers were able to export products to new markets.

In 1847 he became MP for Ipswich, serving until 1868, and then became High Steward of Ipswich from 1875-1882. He is recorded in a memorial stained glass window in Ipswich Library in Northgate Street as one of the great men of Ipswich. In 1884 Felix Cobbold donated a public clock and carillon of chimes to St Clement's Church as a memorial to his father.

Felix Cobbold - Early Years

Perhaps only a minor incident for John Chevallier Cobbold in 1841 was the birth of his ninth child (to survive infancy). Most of the family names had already been bestowed on his earlier children, so the choice of name of Felix perhaps came from the location of his father's holiday cottage on the cliff at Felixstowe. From what we can learn of the young Felix it would appear that he was somewhat in awe of his vigorous, successful father, and his six older brothers. He was educated at Eton College and King's College, Cambridge, where he graduated with a First in Classics in 1865. He appears to have been extremely happy at both Eton and King's, retaining his friends and his interest in his old College all his life. One obituary writer in the East Anglian Daily Times for December 16 1909 wrote:

"He succeeded to the very last Fellowship under the original statutes of Henry VI. The title of Fellow he retained until the end of his life, but the Fellowship had for many years been honorary. Indeed it seems to have been only an excuse for the many generous gifts which he gave to the College. He was called to the Bar by Lincoln's Inn (in 1868) and began to practise, but he soon transferred his activity to Cambridge, where he became one of the Bursars of King's. (1871) In that capacity he took a leading part in bringing about the first of the various extensions of buildings which have enabled the College to house a large proportion of their undergraduates."

Felix at this period chose to stay away from the mansion at Holy Wells and the family businesses to remain in the company of academics in Cambridge and London while he qualified for the Bar. During these years he maintained a close friendship with Henry Bradshaw (d. 1883) who became University Librarian in 1867, and the King's College library retains copies of a number of letters from Felix to Henry.

In 1865 he wrote:

"I am sorry you did not find more MSS at Burleigh as I had hoped you would have been able to clear up a few disputed points as to the moral character of our Virgin Queen Elizabeth - of which, at present, with my very faint remembrances of Froude (?) I am a sceptic. I go to London for the Handel Festival next Monday, to Stow on Tuesday. I shall not go abroad until after the beginning of the Easter Holy Days."

In March 1867 he wrote again to Henry from Berkeley Square in London congratulating him on his appointment, and commented that he was living *"very comfortably"* with Walter Durnford, the son of the Bishop of Chichester, whom he had known at Eton and had also gained a First Class in the Classical Tripos in 1869.

On May 4 1868 he wrote from Wimpole Street to Henry asking for his help in arranging for him to take his MA that year. The letter continues:

"My mother and I are up in London for a fortnight, so that I do not curse my London life just now so much as I usually do at this time and weather of the year. Yesterday I spent the afternoon in Kew Gardens which are truly lovely, and it was pleasant enough sitting under the shade of the magnificent trees there, and pitying the taste of the poor fools and votaries of fashion who were weltering the while in the animal heat and smell of the Zoological Gardens, where there is scarcely a tree up to the casting of shade, and a perfect mille-fleur bouquet of every kind of beast, bird and reptile (man included) the like of which even Noah and his companions were not enjoying when the ark foundered on Mt. Ararat.

Today is cooler but I must confess not so pleasant as I am in a solicitor's office. I am very glad to have had the experience I am now having here, as it will take a great deal ever to induce me to 'go to law', after having seen the very careful way solicitors look after the Bill of Costs as compared with the way they do the rest of their clients' businesses.......Durnford and I jog along very well together........

Yours affectionately,

Felix Cobbold"

King's College, Cambridge

The letters give a picture of a cultured man, fond of music and literature, and the companionship of his intellectual friends. After qualifying, he practised briefly as a lawyer, but in 1871 returned to King's College as bursar, and it seems that he might have remained here had not events in Ipswich drawn him home.

The Cobbold family, 1875

Life began to change in 1875. The year had started well for the family: on 5 January the wife of Felix's elder brother, John Patteson, had a son, Philip Wyndham Cobbold, and in February John Chevallier was elected High Steward of Ipswich. In his letter of thanks to the Mayor and Corporation John confessed that he was not sure what the duties of a High Steward were, and asked for enlightenment, but that there was no doubt that it was a high honour and a final accolade to all his work for the town.

John Patteson (pictured right) had recently also been elected MP for Ipswich, again as a Tory, and in April he was able to urge Parliament to pass the Felixstowe Railway and Pier Bill, which had been rejected by the Lords in 1874. In May he was made alderman for the St Clement's Ward.

Later in the same month, on Whit Monday, John Chevallier lent the ground of the family mansion at Holy Wells to an amalgamated fête of the Odd Fellows and Foresters, and on the following day the 1st Suffolk Rifle Volunteers took over the side shows for their first summer fete. It was a successful day: amid tugs-of-war and bicycle races, a steam hippodrome and roundabouts, the Cobbold family members mingled with the assembled soldiers and their guests. John Patteson was loudly cheered when he appeared in uniform as a Major in the regiment. The 7th Hussars were in barracks, and so came along to lend support to the Volunteers by staging a "Grand Assault of Arms", and at the end of the day the Volunteers' Band Fund benefitted by around £50.

The success and good fortune were soon to end. A few months later John Patteson was dead: on the 3rd and 4th of December he began to feel unwell and Dr. Chevallier from Anglesea Road Hospital was called. John had been due to take the chair of the Licensed Victuallers Association, but he had to cancel the engagement and take to his bed and it soon became clear that he was suffering from a particularly malignant form of scarlet fever. For several days he lingered, and the family had bulletins posted in various parts of the town. Late on 10 December the Ipswich Bulletin was waiting to go to press so they sent a messenger to Cliff House and were told that John was sinking fast. Just after the press deadline a messenger arrived at the paper to say that John had died just before midnight. A long black-edged obituary appeared in the next edition of the paper, describing the general feeling of grief felt in Ipswich. On December 11 most of the shops in the principal streets had their shutters raised...

"and they have not presented such an appearance since the death of the late Prince Consort."

The funeral was an event involving the whole town. It was held in St Mary le Tower, and representatives from all the organisations John was involved with were asked to line up in a nearby street before processing to the church, with a Master of Ceremonies controlling the order of the groups.

It is difficult today to understand fully the immense effect this death had on the community. The newspapers listed some of his interests: not only was he an MP and Alderman but he was Vice Chairman of the Board of Guardians, Captain-Commandant of the 1st Suffolk Rifle Volunteers, and Major of the 2nd Battalion, head of the brewery business, a partner in the banking business, a ship owner, maltster, corn-merchant, Chairman of the Licensed Victuallers... *"and engaged in business in many ways"*. The paper commented that John had retained his popularity even after his election to Parliament, and had a *"bright, happy, genial presence"*. He was only forty-four, and left eight children, the youngest just eleven months old.

Felix Cobbold's return to Ipswich

John Chevallier was devastated by the death of his eldest son, and early in the following year, 1876, he persuaded Felix to return to Ipswich to take over some of the family duties. John Patteson's heir, John Dupuis, was only fourteen, and thus too young to take over as chairman of the brewery, so the work was shared out among the remaining brothers of John Patteson.

One of the numerous concerns of the family was the banking business. Felix and two of his elder brothers became partners in the firm of Bacon's Bank, which became Bacon, Cobbold & Co. (They were later joined by a nephew, the son of Ernest St George.) At Harwich they banked as Cox, Cobbold & Co. and a third firm was called Bacon, Cobbold & Tolemache.

They were later amalgamated under the Capital & Counties Bank, which in turn finally became part of Lloyds Bank. Felix's personal wealth grew steadily, and he seemed destined to spend his life quietly accumulating wealth and helping the family.

However, the death of his father in 1882 became a further turning point in his life. His brother, Thomas Clement, who had earlier worked in the diplomatic service, returned to Ipswich to join Felix in the bank, and to enter Parliament as a staunch Conservative, like John Chevallier and John Patteson. At this point Felix dropped a bombshell: he also wanted to enter politics, but as a Liberal. As one of his obituary writers put it:

"Verily there was a furore when it became known that Mr Felix Cobbold, striking out a line for himself, held opinions which were certainly described correctly in those days as advanced Radicalism. It was the period when agitation for household suffrage was coming to a head, and when the Act was duly embodied on the Statute Book towards the close of 1884, Mr Cobbold was marked as a suitable Liberal champion for one of the Divisions of Suffolk. He consented to stand for the newly-created Stowmarket Division, against the late Sir Thomas Thornhill, the genial Conservative Whip, who had for some years represented the old double-member constituency of West Suffolk."

It was an extraordinary revelation for the family. One can imagine the young Felix attending the many family gatherings at Holy Wells Mansion and listening quietly while his grandfather, his father, and his elder brothers endlessly discussed the state of trade, Ipswich town affairs, and national politics, privately disagreeing with their conclusions, but feeling unwilling to upset his dominant father. With the death of the old man he was at last free, at the age of 41, to make his own views known and start to carve out his own career in public life.

Chapter 2: Liberal politics: agricultural distress and "three acres and a cow."

There appear to be no family papers remaining that describe exactly how and when Felix "outed" himself to the family as a Liberal. While he was living at Holy Wells it would have been difficult for him to entertain political opponents to his brothers, but in his will his father had left him The Lodge at Felixstowe and he moved there in 1885 after extensive renovations (see Chapter 3), and there is documentary proof that he invited people from a wide spectrum of the political scene to visit his new home. However, his work as a banker in Ipswich also brought him into contact with farmers and business men in the town, and Ipswich had a thriving Liberal Association, including such men as Edward Fison, the Grimwade family, R.C. Ransom who also lived in the Holy Wells district, and G.J. Notcutt.

In January 1885 the Liberal Association in Ipswich held a Conference to discuss *"the Seats Bill, the Land Question, County Government and the Affirmation Bill."* Attendees included Joseph Chamberlain, Jesse Collings, and Henry Wyndham West, MP for Ipswich and several other MPs and was held at the Corn Exchange. It was an important event for the town, but was also a national event: a special train ran from Norwich bringing over 100 people, and 2,500 tickets were sold for the Conference sessions. Also present were Lord John Hervey from Ickworth, G.J. Notcutt, Edward Fison, J.H. Grimwade & E. Grimwade and D. Ford Goddard. Chamberlain was due to lay the foundation stone for a new Liberal Assembly room in Brook Street, Ipswich, but on the day he was confined to bed with a tooth abscess at Mr Bulstrode's house, and the stone was laid by someone else.

Felix did not attend according to the newspaper reports: once again family business claimed him. John Patteson's eldest daughter was married at St Mary le Tower on the Thursday of the conference, and the event was attended by the whole Cobbold clan - the Cobbolds, Chevalliers, Jervises, Dupuis etc. and Felix gave his niece £100 as a wedding gift. However, although there is no mention of his attending any of the simultaneous Liberal Conference sessions, it would be strange if Felix did not take this opportunity of meeting all the leading Liberals of his day who were attending a conference within the town.

The period from 1870 had been a particularly difficult time for East Anglian agriculture. A series of bad harvests and foreign competition in the wool trade had led to "the great depression." Eastern farmers saw a rapid fall in the price of their grain, but were slow to adapt to the demand for dairy products. Cries for protection of agriculture were rejected by the Government in favour of free trade. However, Liberal

reformers such as Joseph Chamberlain and Jesse Collings from Birmingham (pictured left[1]) advocated the provision of smallholdings as the solution for the poverty of unemployed agricultural workers, and in the election of 1885 they adopted the slogan of "Three acres and a cow". The plan was for local government authorities to acquire land at a fair value and let it out again to farmers and labourers as allotments or small holdings on terms which would allow the tenant not only to support himself and his family, but also to become the owner of the land in a small number of years. It was a scheme which had already been tried in Ireland, and breaking the stranglehold of the large landowners by local government action would hopefully bring empty farms back into production and end the stream of destitute labourers moving into the cities and towns.

This was one of the burning topics that had been discussed at the Ipswich Conference, and Felix Cobbold became convinced that action must be taken to prevent the continuing decay of the farming community in the area, together with the ensuing crisis in towns crowded with an influx of poor labourers seeking housing and work.

[1] Portrait of Jesse Collings, Birmingham Portraits Collection

The idea was also popular among the agricultural workers, but there was confusion amongst poorly educated labourers as to what the slogan really meant. One letter to the Ipswich Journal from a Mr Wakeman of Blackwell in 1885 asked whether it was only agricultural labourers who were to be given this wonderful gift of three acres and a cow, *"or whether nailers or butchers could also be considered"*.

Suffrage Reform

We have already seen that the Great Reform Bill of 1832 had widened suffrage, but left a substantial part of the population still without a vote and the discontent gave rise to the Chartist Movement. The second Reform Bill in 1867 had extended suffrage to skilled workers in urban areas and the Third Reform Bill of 1884 saw the vote being extended to agricultural labourers. Secret ballots had been introduced in 1872, and the Corrupt Practices Act of 1883 had limited election expenses to £1000 per 5000 voters. At the same time the number of election workers who could be paid also fell, and unpaid workers, especially women, were used for constituency work.

The effect of these reforms was that property owners and employers lost much of their power to secure votes by "influence" over their tenants and employees. This meant that prospective candidates to Parliament needed to attract voters by proposing a framework of ideas put forward by a central party, and party machines emerged, together with modern methods of canvassing. Joseph Chamberlain had founded the National Liberal Federation in 1877, and by 1880 over a hundred local branches, including Ipswich, were affiliated to the organisation.

Felix Cobbold and Stowmarket

Early in 1885, just after the Ipswich Liberal conference, the Irish Bill was defeated in Parliament and the position of the Tory Government under Lord Salisbury became untenable. He stood down but an election, however, had to be delayed as the new electoral rolls were not yet ready and Gladstone became Prime Minister during the interim. The scale of the problem becomes clear when the potential change in the electorate in Suffolk alone is noted: in 1880 there had been 15,335 voters, but in 1885 there were to be approximately 40,000, including the agricultural workers of the County.

By mid 1885 Felix Cobbold had declared his allegiance publicly, announcing his willingness to stand in the forthcoming election, and was adopted as the Stowmarket division candidate, becoming part of a local group of radical Liberals. An article in the Ipswich Journal for August 1 1885 noted that:

"Mr Cobbold was, of course, one of the celebrated 'Peripatetic Gang' comprising Lord John Hervey [whose elder brother was standing as a Conservative candidate in Bury], *Parson Hervey, Francis Seymour Stevenson* [who at the age of 23 was standing in the Eye Division] *Mr R.L. Everett* [a yeoman farmer from Rushmere, standing in the Woodbridge Division], *and Mr Cuthbert Quilter, which carried the fiery cross of advanced Liberalism into every village of Suffolk. The rights of man were to the fore, and Mr Hunter Rodwell* [Stevenson's opponent in Eye] *put his foot into it terribly by stating in a dispassionate reasoning way that men had no more natural rights than pigs or calves. 'He called us pigs and calves,' said one labourer, and the more Mr Rodwell explained, the deeper the muddle became. 'I heerd yer say so,' was the indignant refutation."*

Felix Cobbold as a prospective candidate for Stowmarket

Felix's problem was thus immense. The quiet Cambridge academic, lawyer and banker lacked the extrovert robustness of his father and elder brothers and was totally unused to the rough world of politics, but had the task of convincing the poor labourers of his new constituency that they must come out and vote against the wishes of their employers. Throughout the second half of the year of 1885 he spoke at meetings throughout the area, and initially his inexperience showed. After a meeting at Beyton in late June a letter to the Ipswich Journal complained that one of his election addresses had been incomprehensible...*"It is a matter of question whether the farm labourer has got the remotest idea of what Mr Cobbold was talking about."*

Felix learnt fast. In his speech of July 6 talking about the anti-corn protection laws he said, *"What the Liberals desire to do is to enable the labourers to buy a large loaf at the same price as the Conservatives would make them pay for a small one."* This was a simple analogy thought up by the party machine, reducing the complexities of economic policy to the image of a small loaf and a large one, and Felix also took care to repeat constantly that the Liberals had been responsible for gaining the farm workers their vote.

Another burning issue for the election was the need to reform the Church of England and the possibility of disestablishment. Here Felix differed from Chamberlain who was a firm believer in disestablishment. Felix saw the need for a relaxation of the stranglehold of the power of the Church of England, which excluded non-conformists from the universities and Parliament. He argued at a meeting in Lakeneath: *"The Liberals advocate perfect religious freedom, and maintain that a duly elected person might not be excluded from the House of Commons because he professed a particular religion, or none at all."* This was reform, but not disestablishment.

The campaign was made more difficult for him by personal problems. Nathanael Fromenteel Cobbold, his elder brother and a co-director of the bank, and John Dupuis Cobbold, the current head of the Brewery and thus head of the family, were both Vice Presidents of the Ipswich Conservative Association, and throughout the campaign period they both chaired meetings for opponents. For example, on November 16, John Dupuis held a meeting in St Clement's Ward to introduce Sir W.T. Charley and Murray Ind as Conservative Candidates and in his speech emphasised the strong family connection with the Conservative Party...
    "He remarked that he was much obliged for the kind reception the meeting had given him for it showed that the recollection of his father, (John Chevallier), his uncle (John Patteson), and his grandfather (John Cobbold) had not entirely died away. (Loud cheers and a voice: 'Never will, Sir')."

Another source of irritation must have been the blatant political bias of the newspapers. The Ipswich Journal in particular was so far from believing in the need to present a balanced view that they reported verbatim speeches by Conservatives such as Hunter Rodwell, while the speeches of Felix, Everett, Stevenson and the others were ignored, reported in two lines, or mis-reported. This continued throughout the campaign: the nominations of the Conservative candidate Sir Thomas Thornhill gave his full address and list of supporters together with their addresses and occupations. In contrast the information about Felix states that Felix Cobbold *"of Holy Wells, Ipswich, was thrice nominated, the principal paper bearing the names of R.J. Pettiward, and Mr Lankester Webb."*

Election arrangements - 1885

Arrangements for the elections at this period were complex: nominations were made only a week before voting, and there was a staggered programme of polls throughout the country.

23

In Suffolk the arrangements were:

Constituency	Nominations	Poll	Declaration
Stowmarket	Nov 24	Nov 27	Nov 28
Sudbury	Nov 24	Dec 1	Dec 2
Eye	Nov 26	Dec 3	Dec 4
Woodbridge	Nov 27	Dec 5	Dec 7
Lowestoft	Nov 30	Dec 8	Dec 9

The disadvantage was that events in one constituency were liable to influence the voting in another, but the advantage was that party members were free to help each other once their own election was complete. Felix, whose election took place on November 27 was thus able to help Cuthbert Quilter in Sudbury, and on December 1 rode through Sudbury with Mr and Mrs Quilter and Lord John Hervey, *"in an open carriage and four, with outriders attired in yellow jackets."*

Throughout the county there were riots - in Stowmarket, Ipswich, Long Melford, Lavenham and Clacton, as agricultural workers gathered for the first time to vote, and for weeks after there were reports of court proceedings as rioters were sentenced for their misdemeanours.

Stowmarket Election

Liberals were successful all over the country, but Stowmarket also represented a personal triumph for Felix. It was a Division mostly of large estates owned by Conservative landowners, and included Newmarket with a Conservative racing fraternity. In previous elections the area had returned a strong Conservative majority. With the new electorate, however, things changed. One of Felix's obituary writers in the East Anglian described the day in detail:

"On polling day a local Liberal told the newspaper correspondent that he had met a number of wagons and other carriages carrying voters to the poll, with the horses and men decked with Conservative blue. However, the new voters looked knowingly at the Liberal onlooker as they drove past as if to say, 'We aren't as blue as we look.'"

And so it transpired. *"The Market Place in Stowmarket was filled with a vehement crowd of 'yellows' shouting for Cobbold. 'Where are your colours?' said a voter to a solitary gentleman who ventured in to the*

Market Place wearing a black tie. 'Are you a Liberal?' Such was the popularity of Mr Cobbold that it was difficult for any Conservative to show his head, and Mr Cobbold was returned by a large majority of 1,131."

The election at Stowmarket illustrates clearly the way in which the railway timetable influenced events at this period. Major Higham, who was the chief constable, and his son, had to leave the town by one of the early afternoon trains, and he was escorted to the station by a number of constables for protection amidst a hail of missiles. A further half-score of constables arrived from Bury by a later train to control the situation, along with a group of voters bearing blue placards, but as they tried to march to the poll they were entirely surrounded and a fight ensued, so they were compelled to retreat. The following day when the result was announced, Felix arrived in Stowmarket from Bury on the 3.05pm train, and after making a speech of congratulation and thanks to his party workers he departed on the 5.15pm train for Ipswich.

The results of the poll in Suffolk infuriated the Ipswich Journal. Felix's friend, Everett, had achieved the unthinkable and beaten Lord Rendlesham by just 168 votes, Quilter won Sudbury by 1,457, and the youthful Stevenson beat Hunter Rodwell by 1,996 votes. In Ipswich Jesse Collings and H.W. West were returned again. The Journal declared that democracy had sunk to its lowest ebb in these results: *"Again we say the victories of the Radicals are victories of ignorance over intelligence, of sheer numbers over sound opinions."*

Felix Cobbold, MP for Stowmarket

Felix was now required to spend much of his time in Westminster rather than at his office in Ipswich. However, there were domestic problems to contend with. In January 1886 his brother Nathanael Fromanteel became ill with a cold that turned to jaundice. The Queen's physician, Sir William Jenner, was called, but could not help, and Nathanael died on February 20. His obituary in the Journal said that *"There was no doubt that he would have been chosen Mayor of Ipswich next November so as to represent the Borough in that honourable position in the Jubilee Year of her Majesty's reign, when it is expected that the Mayors of all the important boroughs will receive knighthoods in honour of the national event."*

At the funeral at Westerfield on February 23 there were eleven official carriages from representatives of the Ipswich Water Works, the Mayor and Corporation, and many others, and Felix rode in the third carriage of the procession.

Liberal Party challenges

There were other problems for Felix, although these were not personal but for the Liberal party. As was almost commonplace at this period, the elections were followed by appeals of corrupt practices. Even Felix's own father, John Chevallier Cobbold, had had a petition raised against him in 1857, although he successfully fought off the challenge. Jesse Collings in Ipswich, whose plans for land reform Felix supported ardently, along with West, were accused of malpractice, and on March 2 proceedings were started in the Shire Hall against the two, being held in the Shire Hall instead of the Sessions Court as the Town Hall was not large enough to contain the crowds expected.

The arrival of the judges was an extraordinary event - treated more like a town celebration than the start of a town shame - corrupt election proceedings. The judges were met at the Station by Mayor Grimsey, *"attired in his official robes, wearing the massive gold chain and a cocked hat."* The carriage sent to transport the judges had attendant footmen and coachmen with gold lace round their hats, and in attendance were buglers, twelve policemen marching four abreast, and two Sergeants at Mace.

The court proceedings concentrated on the election practices by employees of the Orwell Iron Works, run by R.C. Ransome, and the Gas Works, run by D. Ford Goddard, both prominent Liberals and neighbours of Felix in the St Clement's Ward. It was alleged that the clerk at the Gas Works and secretary to the St Clements Ward Liberal Association had bribed voters by taking potential voters out to the back yard of the Boiler Maker's Arms Public House and offering them financial inducements to cast their votes, the going rate varying between 1s. 6d, 2s, or even 2s. 6d. in obstinate cases. There was also criticism that Collings had brought a group of Birmingham election workers into Ipswich the day before the election along with a party agent. Chamberlain and Collings had indeed been developing the new art of electioneering in Birmingham in this new age of party politics, but all over the country there must have been similar headshaking as the ways of the old hustings system gave way to new methods.

The case dragged on for days, but finally on April 1 judgement was given against Collings and West, which meant that they were turned out of their seats and could not be re-elected in Ipswich for seven years, although of the one hundred charges made, only eighteen were proved.

In Norwich the Liberal MP was also unseated, although virtually all the charges made against him were not proven. There were, in fact, only three successful petitions for election bribery in 1886, whereas there had been sixteen in 1880.

The town prepared for a by-election. The two original Conservative candidates could not stand so Lord Elcho from Lothian was brought in to stand with Sir Charles Dalrymple. The Liberals included a good friend of Felix's - Lord John Hervey - and Sir Horace Davey, the Solicitor General, who were both strong candidates. Nevertheless the Liberals were defeated and the following day Lord John resigned as President of the Suffolk Institute in the face of threatened mass resignation of all the clerical members of the Institute in protest at Hervey's support for the disestablishment of the church - an issue which Felix had stepped back from in Stowmarket. The whole affair had rocked the Liberal party both in Ipswich and nationally. The National Liberal Club had their funds wiped out by the cost of the trial and the subsequent by-election.

Worse was to follow: in Westminster the Irish Home Rule Bill caused unrest in the party. It became clear that of the thirteen Liberal MPs elected from Essex and Suffolk only Everett and Stevenson remained loyal to Gladstone. The rest, including Felix Cobbold, rebelled, and on June 7

Gladstone was defeated. On June 10 1886 Parliament was dissolved again, so Elcho and Dalrymple had held their seats for less than a month.

Felix decided that he would not stand again in the new election, and returned to his desk at the Bank. Of his friends, Everett was defeated in Woodbridge, Dalrymple and Elcho were re-elected, Cuthbert Quilter standing as a Unionist held Sudbury, and Stevenson, still loyal to Gladstone, held Eye.

For the next few years there was an uneasy truce in Ipswich between the two Liberal camps. An Ipswich Liberal Unionist Association Office was set up at 12, Butter Market in opposition to the Reform Club of the Liberals which remained in Lower Brook Street. Felix joined the Unionists, and remained so until 1898, but, typically, remained friends with many of his former Liberal colleagues, *"treating them with especial courtesy and distinction"*, and apparently continued to pay his Liberal dues. In 1890, Jarrold's Directory of Ipswich lists the Unionist President as T.W. Russell, MP, with Felix as Vice President. Other committee members included W.E. Fison, George Mason JP, Stephen Notcutt, Robert Ransome, with the chairman of the Executive Committee, William Elliston, MD.

Chapter 3: Felix Cobbold of Felixstowe

Felix Cobbold had inherited the cottage called The Lodge in Felixstowe from John Chevallier in 1882. His father had originally rented the property from Sir Samuel Fludyer in 1844 and later bought it as a convenient seaside home while he was in the process of helping to develop the seaside resort. In 1877 the railway had been brought to Felixstowe following the successful lobbying by John Patteson Cobbold, among others, and John Chevallier built hotels and houses along the front, and improved the water supply.

The Lodge had an interesting history: it had originally been a fisherman's hut, but the lieutenant-governor of Landguard fort from 1753-1766, Philip Thicknesse, had acquired it and converted it into a *"charming retreat."* It was at that time about 200 yards from the sea and was approached through a large arch made of septuaria rock. Later the rock was demolished with the intention of improving the view.

FELIXSTOW COTTAGE, near Languard Fort, Suffolk,
the Summer Residence of Governor THICKNESSE,
copied from one of the earliest Productions of GAINSBOROUGH.

By 1882 however, the property needed urgent help if it was to survive. The sea had been gradually approaching the cliffs, and during spring tides reached a point only about 20 yards from the house, and by 1881 was threatening to engulf the whole property. Sparing no expense, Felix had the sea wall and groynes rebuilt to protect the house. The work was so successful that Cobbold Point has been saved for over a hundred years, although recent changes in sea levels have meant that further work is now being carried out.

Felix had decided that he would like to make the house his residence, but it was too small for his needs and he engaged the services of an architect, Mr Cotman, to build a new red brick mansion with just a small plot of grass between the front windows and the low cliff. The work preserved part of the original building, including the room in which Thicknesse had entertained his friend, Gainsborough. By 1885 the work was finished, and Felix somehow found time to leave Holy Wells and move in.

The Lodge at what became known as 'Cobbold's Point', after Felix's renovations

He was justly proud of the house and grounds. Photos reveal the delights of the garden: herbaceous borders, a walled garden, a rose garden with pond and fountain, and pergola-shaded walk. Of the house, an obituary writer for the Suffolk Chronicle wrote:

"The house was furnished with the highest taste and art, not forgetting literature, for Mr Cobbold was one of the best book buyers in Suffolk, and his laden shelves are full of volumes on history, travel, and politics, with a strong dash of East Anglian literature. He was fond of music, gardening, farming, and intellectual company. Many are the distinguished people who have visited The Lodge at Felixstowe - men of all politics and ideas: John Burns the Radical was as welcome as Dr. Jessop the antiquarian, or Herman Biddell, the staunchest of Tories."

The Library also contained many rare Early English volumes and a collection of French works of great value. A second writer tells us that:

"A day at Felixstowe Lodge, or even in the garden or grounds, is a revelation. Money and refinement with an education in keeping, make an English gentleman. As a host Mr Cobbold was all this; and those whom fate has denied the possession of a 'Felixstowe Lodge' may console themselves that there, at least, was an owner who did not abuse the trust."

A third obituary writer, his friend, the Rev. Hervey, wrote that... *"It is indeed grievous to me to think that I shall see his face no more, that I shall never again enjoy the hospitality of his beautiful home at Felixstowe, which he loved so well, and where it was to him such a manifest pleasure to gather his friends and his neighbours around him... Well read, and well informed on many subjects, a frequent traveller, a good judge of pictures and other works of art, he had filled his house with a collection of objects of interest and beauty."*

Felix loved sailing, and joined the Royal Harwich Yacht Club and the Orwell Corinthian Yacht Club. His yawl yacht, Lena, was a well-known sight in Harwich Harbour. The new golf club had its headquarters a short distance from The Lodge round the headland, and, as noted below, was well used by Felix and his guests.

The magnificent dining room at The Lodge

31

The comfortable and elegant drawing room

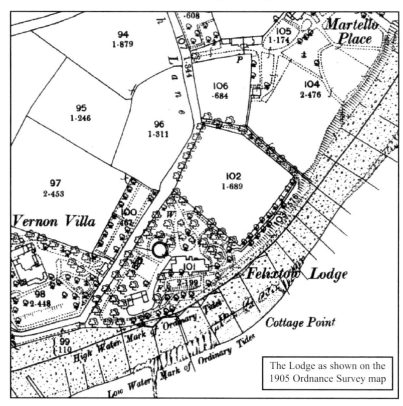

The Lodge as shown on the 1905 Ordnance Survey map

The library

The Pergola

The rose garden
and circular pond,
visible on the map
on page 32.

House parties and friendships

Felix loved entertaining, as the quotes above show, and filled the house with friends, relatives, old friends from College, municipal dignitaries, political enemies and allies, visitors to Felixstowe or whoever else he could get to visit him and admire the house and grounds. He became a member of Felixstowe District Board, and one of his fellow members recalled that Felix often played a little joke by refusing the written requests of the Clerk for help with a scheme, so that the interested parties had to visit him at The Lodge as suppliants, and give him the pleasure of offering them hospitality.

One account of visits to the Lodge comes from the ghost story writer, M.R. James (Montague Rhodes James, 1862-1936) in his autobiographical *'Eton and Kings'* published in 1926:
"It was customary for Cobbold, Willy and Edward Leigh, Richards and Walter Durnford, and Arthur Morton (the well-known private-school master) to assemble at King's about Christmas time. The party, augmented by others, such as Frank Tarver and Ainger, used to move on to the Lodge at Felixstowe and keep New Year there in the height of comfort. When I attained years of discretion, Felix was good enough to include me and others of younger generations in these delightful parties. Those who were not strong enough, or not weak enough, to play golf (which most of them did all day) had a very happy time: Fred Whitting and I would occupy a whole morning over a game of fifty up at billiards: misses and pocketing one's own ball made up the bulk of the score."

What James does not say here is that it became the custom for the group to attend the Nine Lessons and Carols service at King's, drink spiced beer and dine in Hall, and then to retire to a private room where he began the custom of telling a ghost story to his friends. The scene was actually filmed by the BBC in 2000, with Christopher Lee playing the part of James. He is now best known for his skill as a ghost writer, but he had a distinguished academic career, and later became Provost of King's and of Eton. He wrote a number of papers on Early English writers, and catalogued many of the manuscript collections at Cambridge; and it is, perhaps, from him that Felix acquired his own interest, and began his collection of texts.

One of James' most famous stories, *'Oh Whistle and I'll Come to You, My Lad'* was set in Felixstowe. The story features a hotel which is probably the Bath Hotel, built by Felix's father, and mentions ruins near the beach, which in fact are the remains of a Roman fort near the golf course.

Of the others, Sir Walter Durnford (1847-1926) has been mentioned before as a friend when Felix shared rooms with him in London. He was the youngest son of the Bishop of Chichester, the Revd. Richard Durnford, and had had the same academic career as Felix. He later became a master at Eton, and in 1909 became vice-provost at King's. He continued to live there until his death in 1926.

The two Austen-Leighs, William and Edward, are best known as biographers and nephews of Jane Austen. William became a Bursar at King's, as did Felix. William was a fine pianist, and the two brothers are said by James to have been generous donors to King's by supporting the Choral Scholars fund.

Ainger, who also attended the New Year house parties, was perhaps Alfred Ainger (1837-1904) who did not attend Eton, but University College School where he was a friend of the sons of Charles Dickens. In 1856 he matriculated at Trinity Hall, Cambridge, and finally gained an MA in 1865 before entering holy orders and later that year became reader at the Temple, London, remaining there for twenty-seven years. He was known as a good preacher, but was also a writer, a lecturer on literary subjects and an acknowledged expert on Charles Lamb.

The group thus had close ties - shared schooling and college years, academic, literary and musical tastes. The house parties cemented friendships that lasted them all their lives.

Public service and farming

As Chairman of the Felixstowe District Board Felix was asked to lay the foundation stone of the new Town Hall in 1892, a building which reflected the growing size and wealth of the town. (pictured overleaf) The docks had opened in 1887, two years after Felix moved into The Lodge, which provided a new deep water port, able to import and export freight by its connection to the railway. In addition, in 1891 the German Empress had come to stay for a holiday with her children and entourage, and this had set the seal on the town's importance and social standing as a fashionable resort.

Felix had another reason to enjoy his life in Felixstowe. His father had acquired a small farm - Villa Farm, a short distance from The Lodge - afterwards renaming it Lodge Farm and Felix inherited this land along with the house.

Felix Cobbold laying the foundation stone for Felixstowe Town Hall in 1892

For Felix, this became not just a hobby, but a means to learn more about farm management and the local agricultural scene - a subject which held his interest as a politician and follower of Jesse Collings. The farm manager became as much a mentor as an employee, and perhaps helped to advise him when purchasing other farm land. Felix became Chairman of the Suffolk Agricultural Association and even held one meeting at his Felixstowe farm. One visitor to this event commented that Felix clearly did not know much about farming at this stage, but was nevertheless an excellent chairman and was willing to learn.

One incident recalling Felix's generosity was later recalled in the biography of George Seaver, who later became Dean of Ossory in Co. Kilkenny and died in 1976. He recalled that as a small boy he met Felix on the beach at Felixstowe, and recognised him as the...

"...solitary bachelor scholar who lived alone with a household staff of 9 in a palatial mansion fronting the sea....

Violet and I were walking home from the beach one morning when he met us, gave us a humorous grown-ups greeting, shook hands to say goodbye, and left a half-crown piece in mine (in those days quite a large sum). I gazed at it bewildered and embarrassed for a tip was beyond my experience, and handed it back to him with, 'But it isn't mine', and recounted the episode to my mother as soon as I got home. She made me write him a little letter of apology and next morning came a reply, with the coin neatly inserted in a cut card: 'I liked you for refusing my half-crown yesterday, but I like you better now for writing to me about it. Tell me if there is anything you would especially like for a present.' What I longed for most was a set of wood-carving tools, but the cost was prohibitive. Again I consulted my mother and again she suggested - but did not dictate - the line of response. A complete set of wood-carving tools - finest Sheffield steel with beech wood hafts - duly arrived, and so began my first essays in a craft which I kept up for years, till like a fool I gave the tools away and have never ceased to regret it."

He undoubtedly enjoyed his life in Felixstowe, but his heart remained in Ipswich. Thus, in his will he left Felixstowe nothing, which the Chairman of the Urban District Council thought very disappointing. He commented in the memorial meeting that Felixstowe would have *"benefitted greatly from the gift of a park, public hall, free library, or even a drinking fountain and clock on the sea front, but that they must not be envious but feel sure that Mr Cobbold had had his reasons not only for what he did, but also for what he did not do."* He nevertheless said that *"nearly everyone in the room could recall .... a kindly word or genial act of which he was the recipient."*

Felix may not have given the town money, but he had, however, given Felixstowe the benefit of his financial expertise during its expansion, particularly as Chairman of the Board, and had spent money on rebuilding the sea wall at the north part of the town. The bulk of his wealth was to be diverted to other causes, as we shall see.

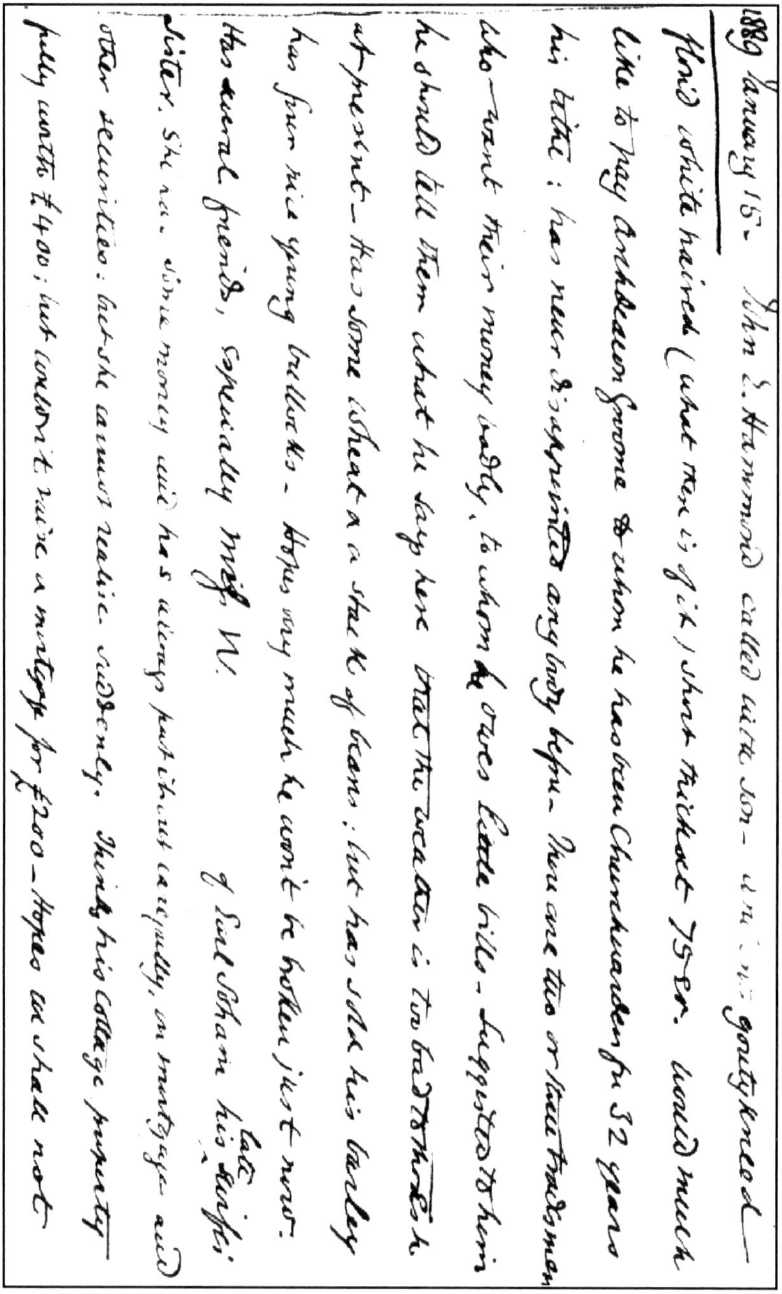

A section of the notebook transcribed on the opposite page

Chapter 4 - Felix the Banker and Citizen

After his withdrawal from Parliament in 1886, Felix needed to refocus his energies and enthusiasm and he returned to his work at the Bank. A notebook of his, written between the years 1886-1893, is held in the archives of Lloyds Bank which records some of his customers, which included the Carr Street Improvement Company, the Woodbridge Rifle Volunteer Corps, R & W Paul, and Parknold & Co. which later became part of Fisons. Reading through the pages, it becomes clear that his job gave Felix an insight into the financial pulse of the town, and of the surrounding countryside.

The book shows the very personal nature of banking, since many of the decisions Felix makes are based on his judgement of the men sitting before him. One account describes a worried farmer visiting his office as an *"ancient gouty-kneed florid white-haired (what there is of it) short thickset 75er. Would much like to pay Archdeacon... to whom he has been churchwarden for 32 years his tithe; has never disappointed anybody before. There are two or three tradesmen who want their money badly, to whom he owes little bills - suggested to him he should tell them what he says here that the weather is too bad to thresh at present. - Has some wheat, a stack of beans, but has sold his barley. Has four nice young bullocks. Hopes very much he won't be broken just now..."* (see opposite)

The notebook also gives a glimpse of the problems of banking at this time. One customer intended to depart to Woodbridge by the afternoon train. However, at ten to four he produced a cheque to the amount of £61 13s. from Gurney's Bank which he wanted cashed, which caused a flurry as the decisions had to be made before four-thirty. Once again the train timetables were dominating Felix's life.

There was a darker side to his life: in 1886 his brother Nathanael Fromenteel had died, aged only 47. Of the others, John Patteson, the eldest son, had died in 1875 aged 44, The third son, Thomas Clement had entered the diplomatic service, but then left the service and came back to Ipswich to work as a partner in the Bank, but died in 1883, aged 49. The fourth son, Herbert Wilkinson was born in 1835 but died in 1852 aged 17, and the fifth son, Temple Francis, had been born in 1836 and survived only to 1837. Thus, by 1886 Felix had only two brothers out of seven still surviving: Henry Chevallier and Major Ernest St George.

Felix must have begun to feel that he was perhaps on borrowed time: at the age of 45 he was already older than John Patteson had been at his death and he had not married and produced children like his brothers. It appears that at about this time he began to acquire parcels of land throughout East Suffolk, planning to pursue his dream of providing smallholdings and allotments for impoverished agricultural workers. His job afforded him unique information about land sales and also provided daily reminders of the dire state of the farming community.

Christchurch Mansion

One matter which came to his attention in 1892 was the sale of the estate of William Neale Fonnereau, which was put on the market at a price of £50,000. The people of Ipswich were consulted in a referendum as to whether the town should purchase the estate, which included Christchurch Park and mansion, but they rejected such an expensive project. Accordingly in 1894 a Syndicate bought the estate for only £36,000 as building land. In June they sold 284 rods abutting Bolton Lane, and shortly after sold land on Park Road, whereupon houses began to arise on both sites. At that point the Town and Corporation realised that their decision had been short sighted, and Ipswich risked losing amenity land close to the centre of the town. Accordingly, the Council raised £16,500 and bought fifty-one acres of the Park. This, however, left Christchurch Mansion itself and the ground in front and to the west of it, abutting Fonnereau Road and Clark's Arboretum, in the hands of the Syndicate. The group now drew up plans to demolish the Mansion and build a row of terraced houses.

Christchurch Mansion as painted by Leonard R. Squirrell

At this point Felix intervened. On 23 October the Mayor received a letter from him:

"Dear Mr Mayor,
Having contracted to purchase Christchurch House with the land adjoining and studio, as shown on a plan which will be submitted to you, I desire to offer the property to the inhabitants of Ipswich as a free gift, subject to certain conditions.

One condition which I make is that the purchase of the park, which the Town Council have agreed to make subject to the consent of the Local Government Board, is carried through.

My other conditions are that the main structure of the house be preserved in its integrity, and that in adapting the building to such purposes as the town may decide, the internal fittings, by which I mean the wainscotting of the hall, and of the principle rooms and passages, the marble pavement of the hall, and the main staircase, be retained as far as practicable.

I shall be much obliged if you will submit this offer to the Town Authorities.
Felix T. Cobbold."

The offer was gratefully accepted, and the Park and Mansion were thus saved to become town amenities.

However, the use to which the Mansion was to be put became the next question facing the Council. The Borough Technical Instruction Committee had been running classes in the High Street Museum Buildings, but they had grown in popularity and outgrown their accommodation and it was proposed and agreed that they should move to the Mansion. Thus, for the next ten years therefore, it became a technical college. On the passing of the Education Act in1889, however, the new Education Board took over responsibility for the classes and they were moved to a new Secondary School on Tower Ramparts.

Once again the Mansion was empty, and Felix was consulted to determine his wishes. The Museum Committee proposed that it should be used as a local Archaeological Museum and Picture Gallery, thus relieving pressure on the High Street premises. Felix agreed, and took a close personal interest while the project was put into effect, an interest which he maintained until the end of his life. In his will he then left twenty thousand pounds, the interest of which were to be used to purchase pictures and works of art and enable further restoration of the building.

41

Fore Street Baths

Felix made further bequests to the town around this time: in 1894, just before the Christchurch gift, he also gave the site of St Clement's Baths, Fore Street, to the town along with a sum of £1,200 for the building. He was invited to give a speech at the opening, but his words must have given some embarrassment to the Council:

"I have been told that in some aristocratic towns (I am glad Ipswich is not one of them) there are different classes: the first class ladies one day, the first class gentlemen another, and then at the end of the week, when the water is dirty, the poor are admitted."

Fore Street Baths soon after opening

As Felix probably knew full well, these were indeed the arrangements which the Council had decided upon for the management of these baths, but even the speech failed to shame them into amending the rules. The incident, however, gives a typical example of Felix's dry sense of humour.

Chapter 5 - Mayoral Year and the Diamond Jubilee Celebrations, 1897

After his generosity to the town it was decided that Felix should become Mayor of Ipswich during the Diamond Jubilee year, in spite of the fact that he was not an alderman and therefore not normally eligible. There was some poignancy for Felix in this choice, because, as we have noted in Chapter 2, it had been previously planned that Nathanael Fromanteel should be given this honour, but his death had intervened.

It was a busy time: each week he sat as a magistrate in the Police Court and was involved in numerous other civic duties in Ipswich, and in Felixstowe he remained as treasurer of the Felixstowe and Walton Ratepayers' Association. He became one of the first members of East Suffolk County Council, but as his family bank held the treasureship of the Council he resigned almost at once to prevent a conflict of interests.

The town felt some trepidation at the prospect of the forthcoming festivities, as previous celebrations had not been as successful as they had hoped and had drained the town's finances. Accordingly, in April, Felix summoned a public meeting in the Council Chamber of the town hall to consider the nature of the celebrations. The town had already recently dispatched a considerable amount of money to India, and bought Christchurch Park and the feeling was that it was not right to spend much money on this occasion. One proposal was that a dispensary for the poor should be opened.

Felix finally suggested that the town should raise money to repair and enlarge the Ipswich and East Suffolk Hospital in Anglesea Road and offered to lead the list with a donation of £1000. However, he also announced that he would himself pay for a programme of festivities. It was therefore agreed with some relief that the Mayor's Fund should build a 'Jubilee wing' at the Hospital, and Felix himself should fund the town celebrations in June.

Felix's proposal followed a long family association with the hospital. His father had been one of the founders of the hospital, becoming the first Treasurer and Secretary of the board, and many early meetings were held at Holy Wells Mansion. Although he later gave up the Secretaryship, he remained as Treasurer until two years before his death. John Patteson, Felix's elder brother, also took a close interest in the hospital, and after his death the children's wing, the Cobbold ward was

43

built in his memory, and the Patteson ward opened. At this time Thomas Clement Cobbold, another brother, became a Vice President. Felix had joined the Board in 1886 and later became President.

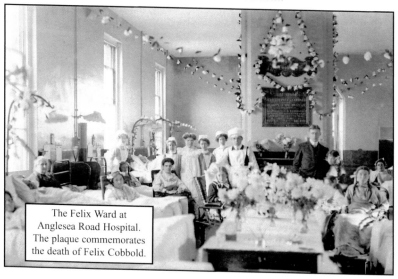

The Felix Ward at Anglesea Road Hospital. The plaque commemorates the death of Felix Cobbold.

John Dupuis Cobbold offered to donate £500 to buy land at the racecourse as an additional resource for the town so that the young people at the east end of the town would benefit, and this offer was, of course, also received with gratitude. The gift, made on 12 May 1897, was of over eleven acres for a public playground in Nacton Road which could be used for football in winter and cricket in summer.

Time was short, but a Jubilee committee was formed and began a series of meetings to discuss arrangements, with Felix in the chair. On 12 May it was agreed that the committee should be empowered to erect *"such booths, refreshment stalls, posts and fencing as they may think necessary"* and be given permission for a display of fireworks in Christchurch Park on 22 June.

Meanwhile the Mayor's Fund for the hospital continued to grow: by May 19 it had raised £2,508, and by early June this had risen to £8,267. Other members of the Cobbold family were extremely generous: John Dupuis gave £500, Philip Cobbold donated £1,000, Lady Evelyn Cobbold and John Murray Cobbold each gave £500. By the end of the year £8,717 could be given to defray the cost of building the Victoria Wing with its Felix ward, and also to refloor the male and female surgical wards, and the 'sanitary arrangements' reconstructed.

The celebrations

On May 25 the 1st Volunteer Battalion of the Suffolk Regiment held a concert at Masonic Hall in honour of the Queen's Birthday, and Felix was among the guests. However, the climax of the celebrations came later. On June 20 the Mayor and Corporation attended a service at St Mary le Tower, on June 22 a gala day in the park for townspeople was held, on June 23 a giant party for school children was also held in the park, and the following day a dinner for over-63 year-olds was given at the Corn Exchange and Public Hall - all funded by Mayor Cobbold.

Volunteers marching

The first of the three days of celebrations, the Party in the Park, was a great success. The programme of events included races, a bowling tournament and four bands, which played throughout the day. At 11.45 am the 1st Volunteer Battalion fired a salute, and at 3.00 pm there was a Military Tournament. In addition there was a steam circus, a tunnel railway, and a quoits tournament, and, of course, the 'booths, refreshment stalls etc.' which had been agreed on May 12. At dusk there was a grand firework display, and the Town Hall was lit up at 10.00 pm by gas jets illuminating the columns and coloured lights on the roof.

The children's party on the second day had been organised with military precision. Two thousand children under five years old were to be provided with tea at their schools, but a staggering 10,650 children were invited to a celebration in the park. The planning committee, presided over by Mr J. Hepburn Hume, Clerk of the School Board, included eight members nominated by the Ipswich Teachers' Association. They had advised the Mayor that a similar celebration held in 1887 had had catering problems, and on this occasion it was agreed that all the catering should be placed in the hands of one company.

On June 1 the East Anglian Daily Times reported that the weight of the cake alone would amount to over 2 tons 7cwts, and 1330 gallons of tea would be served. The weight of the rolls and butter would equal the amount of cake, so that the whole would weigh close on 5 tons. It was calculated that *"if the slices of cake were placed singly one above the other it would make a column more than twice the height of the famous Eiffel Tower. The flat rolls similarly placed would considerably overtop that celebrated structure. The portions of cake and buttered rolls were to be placed in 10,650 paper bags in 50 large crates, one to each school department, the average weight of the crates being 2 cwt."*

Further precautions had been taken by the committee in preparing the undertaking that the baking of the rolls should be carried out within a specified number of hours before the tea so that they would all be fresh, and a steam traction engine was hired to drag the crates to Christchurch Mansion. (see below)

The day began well. The children were marched in columns into the park at 2.00 pm to begin a programme of games before the tea, many groups carrying banners with slogans like *"Long Life to Our Mayor."* However, between three and four o'clock the *"long threatening storm broke with tremendous violence. The lightening was almost incessant and*

very fierce, and the peals of thunder terrifying, while the rain eventually came down in torrents." One can imagine the consternation of the teachers trying to control 10,650 over-excited children in such a storm. Some were apparently quite unphased and strolled about with apparent unconcern, but many were terrified. Fortunately for Felix and his helpers, the Suffolk Agricultural Show had been held in the Park a few days earlier, and the sheds covered with waterproof canvas were still in place, so the children were gathered under these structures. It was noted that the Mayor himself assisted in this work, *"evincing great solicitude for the safety of his little guests."*

Many children invaded Christchurch Mansion itself. In the ensuing mayhem, arrangements for serving the food were somewhat hindered, and one newspaper commented rather sourly that they could have been served better *"if they had shown a little more consideration."* One can imagine that over 10,000 children on a holiday from schoolwork, half soaked by a cloudburst, and wanting their tea would have been noisy and overexcited, and confusion was to be expected. However, the four hundred and thirty teachers eventually managed to serve the food and drinks, helped by Mrs J.P. Cobbold, Mrs J. White-Jervis, Miss Jervis, and Mrs N.H. Cobbold, Felix's female relatives recruited for the day. At 6.00 - 7.30 pm, *"eccentric balloons"* were released, and the party was finally over.

The Old People's Dinner on June 24 was a more sober affair, but enjoyed by the 1,250 that were able to attend the meal. A further 1,000 old people were unable to come but they were given 2s. each *"orders on tradesmen"* by Felix to enable them to buy a small treat.

Children's picnic day. Note the agricultural tent in the background

Felix arranged for flowers to decorate the tables to be sent up from his house in Felixstowe, and the menu included roast and boiled beef and mutton, new potatoes, steamed plum pudding, and strawberries, oranges and apples. Beer and lemonade were also served.

Celebrations in Christchurch Park, June 1897 for the Diamond Jubilee of Queen Victoria

Children's party day in Christchurch Park, with the steam engine in the foreground delivering the food

The whole celebrations must have been hugely expensive for Felix, but provided entertainment and a memorable few days for Ipswich. In addition, the Hospital gained the new Jubilee Wing in due course financed by the Mayor's Fund.

Felix was also involved to a minor extent in the Felixstowe Town celebrations, as an important resident of the town. On April 24 1897, the Town held a meeting attended by Felix to discuss their own celebrations. As Ipswich had agreed three weeks earlier to add the Jubilee Wing to the hospital, Felix suggested that Felixstowe should endow a bed at Anglesea Road Hospital, although an alternative proposal had been made that a Cottage Hospital should be set up in Felixstowe itself. Finally, Felix's proposal was accepted, in addition to the erection of a shelter in the Town.

The Cobbold Loving Cup

As Felix's mayoralty drew to a close there were two more events of note. On 9 November, prior to a Council meeting, Felix invited members to meet with him in the Town Clerk's Office. He then presented them with a silver loving cup and stand bearing the following inscription: *"A loving cup. The gift of Felix Thornley Cobbold, Mayor, in Queen Victoria's Great Jubilee year, AD 1897"*

49

The Council immediately passed a motion that *"The thanks of the people of Ipswich, by the voice of the Town Council as their elected representatives, be cordially given to Felix T. Cobbold Esq. for the eminent services he has rendered to the community during his ever memorable year of office as Mayor of the Borough."*

In April 1896 the Council had commissioned a portrait of Felix by the Hon. John Collier and for the final event of 1897 there was a gathering in the Great Hall of Christchurch Mansion for the unveiling of the picture, with Edward Packard presiding, and the presentation made by Lord John Hervey, Felix's old friend. Lord John mentioned that nearly all the subscriptions had been collected before Felix became Mayor, with eight hundred and ninety subscribers.

The portrait, which still hangs in the Mansion, shows Felix sitting in a large armchair beside the ornate wooden fireplace in the lounge of Felixstowe Lodge.

Chapter 6 - The Khaki Election of 1900

In 1898 a by-election was called in South Norfolk as the sitting MP, Francis Taylor, decided to retire. A candidate was required quickly and as the first choice, Sir William Brampton Gurdon, could not be found even though *"the telegraph was used,"* Mr Soames, who had previously stood unsuccessfully for Ipswich, took his place. To the surprise of the Liberal party managers, Felix Cobbold also offered his services, but he was a few hours too late as Soames had already begun campaigning. Nevertheless, the event marks Felix's return to the Liberal camp.

In 1899, the newspapers were filled with articles on South Africa, and on October 9 the Boer War began. Local politicians such as Stevenson, Pretyman, Quilter and Everett vied with each other in making speeches supporting the Government. Day by day in October the papers listed details of the transports, and reports of the fond farewells as men departed from Ipswich and Colchester. Speeches from General Gatacre to the troops, *"recently commanding in Colchester,"* were reported, as was his defeat in battle.

On October 27 1899 Parliament was prorogued, but an election was not called until September 1900 which gave time for plans to be laid. In July of 1900 the Liberals in Ipswich suffered the loss of J.S. Allport, the agent. He had been a good friend of Felix, who had appreciated the fact that he had continued to pay his dues, and refused to stand as a Unionist against his erstwhile colleagues. The funeral on July 6 was well attended, and the list of mourners gives a good indication of the current local party membership: it includes Mr S.A. Notcutt, Mr C. Ransom, Mr T. Keeble of the Woodbridge Liberal Association, and Mrs Daniel Ford Goddard, wife of the MP, who was listed as being President of the Ipswich Women's Liberal Association. Felix attended and sent a wreath.

In September when the election was finally called the Government faced increasing expenses and problems with the conduct of the war. Felix was offered a chance to stand for Ipswich, along with Sir Daniel Ford Goddard, but he declined in favour of the more demanding constituency of the Woodbridge Division - a seat which covered an area from Aldeburgh in the north to East Bergholt with Stratford St Mary and Brantham in the south. It was a strange decision: Felix's personal popularity in Ipswich was very high, and he would almost certainly have been elected. The Woodbridge seat, by contrast, covered part of Ipswich, but also covered the Conservative towns of Woodbridge, Aldeburgh, and

East Bergholt. However, it was hoped that the vote of the agricultural labourers in the outlying villages would be more than enough to sway the result, as they had at Stowmarket in 1885. Felix's place in Ipswich was taken by a Mr Buxton.

The campaign, and dirty deeds

The campaign began with the usual preliminary skirmish of published election addresses. The Conservative candidate for Woodbridge was once again Captain E.G. Pretyman, not only an ex-soldier, but the owner of an estate of 20,000 acres, living at Orwell Park, Ipswich. His address of 26 September showed his firm support for the war. *"After twelve months of severe fighting, the war forced upon us by the Boer Republics, has been brought to a successful issue, and our predominance in South Africa is now assured. Such desultory opposition as still exists can only be prolonged in the hope that there may be a change of Government here, and that the firm policy of the present Ministry may give place to that other policy of surrender which has cost us so dearly both in South Africa and in the Sudan... I shall, if again returned to Parliament, give my unswerving support to such administrative measures as will compel obedience to British rule throughout South Africa."*

Pretyman's sanguine announcement of victory fitted the mood of the moment. The public were jubilant at the successful relief of Ladysmith on February 28, and of Mafeking on 17 May, and the organised resistance of the Boers to the British invasion was not to start for several more weeks. A spirit of jingoism prevailed and support for "our boys" was everywhere apparent.

Felix's address, by contrast, showed that he was not so sympathetic, and saw clearly the military problems being revealed by the campaign.

"When the British Colony of Natal was invaded by the armed forces of the South African Republics, the only course open to us was to drive the enemy from our Dominions. But the conduct of the Government in their negotiations with President Kruger has justly merited the scorn of all true patriots, as it has earned the hatred of the other nations of Europe against us. The Government's unpreparedness for the inevitable war has completed our disgrace in the eyes of Europe."

He went on by accusing the Tories of having an ulterior motive for the war: *"...we have it on the authority of Mr Chamberlain himself, that it is the ordinary strategy of the Tories to distract the people's attention from Home Affairs to the complications of Foreign Policy..."*

If this speech succeeded in causing anger among the voters supporting the war, worse was to follow. In the 1885 election he had drawn back from supporting the disestablishment of the Church of England, but his views had now hardened.

"The present position of affairs in the Established Church shows us that it is powerless as a bulwark of defence against Sacerdotalism and the idolatries and superstitions in withstanding which our forefathers in East Anglia fought and many laid down their lives. I believe that the true remedy for these disorders lies in Disestablishment and Disendowment, care being taken to maintain and strengthen the Protestant basis upon which the Church was originally established."

The area had a strong Methodist following, particularly among agricultural workers, and the address would have found favour with this section of his readers, but the churchmen of the constituency must have been choking over their breakfast toast.

Felix had thrown down the gauntlet, but the campaign proved to be even harder than he anticipated. At the early meetings he was rudely heckled by a Mr Harrison who was later to be revealed as a paid agent of the Conservatives. Felix denounced him as such in a speech of September 30, and Pretyman denied it on October 1, but after a meeting in Felixstowe, the Tory agent admitted his responsibility and the offending man was silenced.

Another paid agent was discovered: the gardener to the Rector of Clopton, a certain Henry Mendham, was taken to the Woodbridge Division of the High Court on October 4 by Felix for having repeatedly alleged at various places in the constituency that *"Mr Cobbold was an Atheist, and did not believe in God."* Felix filed an affidavit denying the charges and asked for an injunction to be served on Mr Mendham restraining him from making further malicious statements. Mendham did not come to court, but was represented by a solicitor who said that his client undertook not to repeat the statements, so the judge did not actually impose a restraining order. This legal representation in itself is revealing, suggesting that his defence was being paid for either by the Rector of Clopton or by the Tory agent.

53

Yet another paid agent appeared in the guise of a retired sailor who had been hired to tour pubs attacking Felix's policies. Felix met him in the Dog Public House in Grundisburgh, *"trying to bamboozle the agricultural labourers whom he may happen to meet by reading extracts from Tory literature... and by defending the mismanagement of the Tory Government in the South African war."* Felix called him a *"Tory locust."* The sailor at first denied his employment by the Tory party, but next day admitted to Felix's agent that it was true, and showed him a list of the other pubs he was supposed to visit.

There were other problems. Felix was attacked by Pretyman for his change of party in 1886. On October 3, Pretyman said: *"Mr Cobbold has expressed various opinions, and what he said today might be very different from what he might say on the morrow... The very bills he issued were half blue and half yellow, and after all, what the labourers liked was a man who stuck to his colours."* (Cheers.)

However, there was one speaker, chairing a meeting in Hintlesham in October 1900, who came to his rescue:
"Mr Cobbold was born into a conservative family. He couldn't help that, but, as soon as he began to read and think for himself he became a Liberal, and has been a Liberal from conviction ever since. A man who, by the logic of facts and the lessons of history, felt compelled to sever himself from old family traditions, and to take a different position at great personal sacrifice, deserves the respect of everybody as an honest man."

The speech must have been welcome to Felix, who was clearly feeling bruised by the number of attacks he was experiencing. The comment about the 'great personal sacrifice' is interesting as it is one of the only references which confirms the family problems that must have arisen from Felix's Liberal stand. Another possible problem at this point was that Lord Kitchener of Khartoum was in fact the grandson of the Rev. John Chevallier, and thus a relative of Felix's. His anti-war stance must have angered his brothers.

At this Hintlesham meeting Felix once again revealed his extreme Radicalism: after speaking of the hard lot of the labourers he commented: *"If the labourers would only combine as Mr Joseph Arch advised them to do in 1872 their position in life would be still further improved."*[1]

---

[1] Joseph Arch had been the leader of the agricultural workers during the great "lockout" of 1874, who founded the National Agricultural Union. The movement had been particularly strong in East Suffolk, so listeners at this meeting must have known from personal experience the terrible years of the lockout and the subsequent distress as thousands left the land for good.

By thus supporting Trade Unionism Felix was clearly taking a gamble that support from the agricultural workers would once again propel him into Parliament, but he was simultaneously antagonising all the farmers and landowners of the constituency - a dangerous stance.

The anomalies of the political system of the day become apparent at this point. On October 3, the day of Pretyman's speech reported above, polling was taking place in Ipswich, and the numbers were so close that while Goddard was elected, Buxton trailed behind, and the second MP became the Conservative Dalrymple. If Felix had agreed to stand here, his personal popularity might have resulted in the few extra votes required to return him to Parliament.

In the paper of October 6 which reported the meeting at Hintlesham a news item appeared which confirmed Felix's dedication to the ideal of land reform. Applicants were invited to apply to acquire acres in a site known as Arnold's Field at Hadleigh owned by Felix Cobbold which was being divided into smallholdings. Lord Carrington had written an article a few years earlier describing his experiment in setting up smallholders on land in Buckinghamshire and Lincolnshire, and Felix had now acquired 750 acres, of which Arnold's Field was the latest addition, to do likewise. The land was *"to be let to working men in plots of one acre each, rent 20s per acre, free of rates and tithes."*

Furthermore, it was made clear that Felix would look favourably on any man who tried to buy his acre by setting the price at £18 per acre, so that the purchaser would pay 28s per year for 12 years, with an additional 5s for tithes and rates, and at the end of this period would own the land. It would be unfair to conclude that this was just a political ploy to win votes, although the gesture contrasted with Pretyman's ownership of a large estate which Felix attacked in speech after speech as being detrimental to the well-being of the countryside.

Woodbridge polling day

Polling eventually took part in the Woodbridge Constituency on October 10 at twenty-seven different stations. In Woodbridge itself, the appearance was all blue. *"A majority of the residents wore blue rosettes, some dogs were blued all over, and the talk was mainly in favour of a blue candidate."* Furthermore, according to the East Anglian, the Tories had *"no end of helpers",* and a constant stream of carriages lent by their many supporters ferried people to the poll.

In contrast, the Liberals had a good number of helpers, but apparently had carriages only from Ford Goddard, MP, and Sir W.B. Gurdon, MP, although a Mr Rowlands of the Thoroughfare lent some wagons and traps which were useful *"for the accommodation of labourers from outlying parishes."*

This has a strange ring: Felix was limited to the amount he could spend on the campaign to £1,000, but if there had really been a transport problem he could have hired carriages for the day, or lent Cobbold carriages, so the report may indicate biased reporting.

Elsewhere there were dirty tricks, and the paper clearly revealed its bias. In East Bergholt, it reported that houses of known Liberal sympathisers, and the Liberal headquarters itself, had been daubed with blue paint overnight, while at Aldeburgh campaign posters had been painted blue. Here, it commented *"the humorous part"* was that the local workers had suspected trouble and had mounted guards on other nights, but on the eve of election they had *"been caught knapping."* (sic.)

The only retaliation recorded was at Wickham Market where the tent erected in an orchard to house the Tory HQ near the election station was surrounded by... *"a party of boys. After indulging in howls and groans they pelted the temporary structure with stones and rotten eggs until the police appeared."*

Woodbridge results day

The election result was announced the following day at Woodbridge at about mid-day. A crowd gathered on Market Hill, and the East Anglian reported with heavy humour that *"the irrepressible Mendham* (the gardener/agent who had been taken to court by Felix) *came in bearing a bouquet of flowers and the report was - though this is not a matter upon which an affidavit can be made - that he 'came a cropper' off his bicycle in trying to ride through the people."* In the interval before the announcement, *"patriotic songs were lustily chanted, and two ex-buglers of the Volunteers added to the noise and tumult."*

The result of the election was that Captain Pretyman had gained 5,089 votes, and Felix had only 4,437. Lady Beatrice Pretyman was then presented with a bouquet of red, white and blue flowers - perhaps those brought by Mendham from the Clopton garden, and *"the carriage was dragged round the town by scores of working men and for some time nearly all Woodbridge indulged in a demonstration of enthusiasm."*

56

For once Felix displayed uncharacteristic anger at the end of this wounding campaign. He had yet another lawsuit pending, so that at the Liberal Party HQ in New Street after the result he complained, *"I have a character at stake. They chose to put the issue on personalities, for on our side we never uttered one word that could be stated to be personal during the whole of the contest."*

Someone suggested tactfully that he should bury the hatchet, at which Felix retorted, *"Yes, we will bury the hatchet, and bury it in the most appropriate place. This attack on my personal character... must be defended in a proper Court of Justice."*

However, before retiring once more to his life of banking and local affairs in Ipswich and Felixstowe, Felix went on to pledge his services again if the party should need him in the next election.

Woodbridge Market Place

.

Chapter 7 - The Final Years and the 1906 Election
Private and public affairs

Felix returned once again to his desk at the Bank after his defeat in Woodbridge, and resumed his various duties in Ipswich and Felixstowe, but must have felt a sense of anticlimax. He took a trip to America and apparently visited the Mormons in Utah. Several ladies of his family had moved to Felixstowe - a Miss Cobbold in Constable Road, a Miss J. Stokesly Cobbold in Barton Road, and a Mrs Cobbold in the Undercliffe. By this time the town had a yacht club, a croquet club, and a cricket club, a choral society, a literary society, a hockey club and even a swimming club. After the visit of the German Empress in 1896 there was a constant stream of smart visitors, and by 1904 the town boasted the giant Bath Hotel built by John Chevallier standing in six acres of land, the Felix Hotel, the Grand Hotel, and the Orwell Hotel on the cliffs. It was a pleasant town to live in, and Felix enjoyed a stream of guests whenever he was at home. His obituary in the East Anglian Daily Times says: *"the visitor was soon aware that his host was a cultivated gentleman of wide knowledge and literary tastes. The library, in which its owner took so especial a pride, contains many rare early English volumes, while there is, too, a fine collection of French works of great value. The house itself is a perfectly appointed home, and the extensive gardens, made out of the most unpromising materials, and only safeguarded from the encroaching sea by a retaining wall of great strength, rank high among the pleasure grounds of East Anglia."*

The obituary also notes that he supported *"much of the educational work of the borough, and his purse has been at the disposal of many young people who gave evidence of striking ability. To what extent his generosity was accorded private individuals can never be known - he did not reveal to others the manifold gifts he bestowed."* Another obituary from the Chronicle commented in the same way that *"His generosity was great and he never let his right hand know what his left gave away. When he gave something, even for a public object, he generally finished up with a quiet remark, 'You don't want to talk about it.'"*

He could have spent the rest of his days in the town and at his desk at the bank, but his ambition for public life was still keen. Moreover, the world outside his small circle was changing dramatically

In January 1901 Queen Victoria died, and the Edwardian era began. In South Africa the Boers were not beaten as easily as had been expected, and in March 1901 began their guerrilla warfare, which the Generals found difficult to counteract because it did not follow the rules of war as they interpreted them, and for the first time troops from Australia and New Zealand were mobilised to support the British Army. As attacks began on isolated units, the British army responded by destroying farms and moving the civilian population, including women and children, into badly run concentration camps which caused immense suffering. A peace treaty was finally signed in May 1902 by the Treaty of Vereeniging, but the Boers were given three million pounds to restock and repair farms destroyed by the British.

The Liberal Party felt vindicated in their opposition to the war: the disgraceful treatment of the women and children, and the cost in terms of money and men left a bad taste in the mouth. The war had cost over two million pounds, and had involved over 450,000 troops.

To recoup some of the money, in 1904 the Government decided to import Chinese labour to the Transvaal to reopen the gold mines - a move opposed by Australia, Canada and New Zealand, and in England by the Liberal Party.

One domestic issue concerning the Liberals was the passing in 1902 of the Education Act which abolished 2,568 school boards and handed their duties to local boroughs or county councils as Local Education Authorities. At the same time Church of England schools were given LEA funding. Nonconformists, together with the Liberals and the new Labour Representation Committee, were outraged, and many refused to pay school taxes. The National Passive Resistance Committee was formed, and by 1906 over 170 men had gone to prison, including 60 Primitive Methodists, 18 Baptists, 40 Congregationalists and 15 Wesleyan Methodists. Not only were their taxes being used to support Church of England schools, and conformist religious education in LEA schools, but teachers were subject to religious tests.

Back to the Hustings

In November 1905, Balfour resigned, but did not ask the King for the dissolution of Parliament. Instead the Liberal Campbell-Bannerman took control of Parliament on December 5, but then began to prepare for an election.

In December Felix was again adopted as a candidate for the Liberal Party, but this time he partnered Daniel Ford Goddard in Ipswich, and Everett returned to the Woodbridge Division in his place. Captain

Pretyman was again adopted by the Conservatives for Woodbridge, sponsored by John Dupuis Cobbold.

By early January 1906 election fever was in evidence. Felix Cobbold and Goddard published their election manifestos in the East Anglian Daily Times on the same day, and, highlighted the main issues: Chinese slavery, the Education Act, high taxes, and Free Trade, Peace, Retrenchment and Reform. I will quote this address in full as it contains all the major themes of Felix's concerns at the end of his life.

"To the Freemen and Electors of the Borough of Ipswich
Fellow Townsmen,
The times which have tried the hearts of men are past. The Tory Ministers, not daring to face another Session of Parliament, have fled ignominiously from their posts, and have been succeeded by a body of Liberal politicians whose advent to power has been received with universal satisfaction throughout the country. It rests with the Electors to secure for themselves an era of Peace, Retrenchment and Reform by returning to Parliament supporters of the new Government.

Of all the interests which make for the welfare of a nation the greatest is Peace. During the past fifty years our country has been engaged in numerous wars and aggressive frontier attacks at the outposts of our Empire, all of which might have been avoided by Arbitration, and a spirit of Conciliation. During the past ten years the wars which have marked the course of the Tory Government, and of which they make their boast, besides the awful loss of life, have swollen the National Debt by upwards of 150 million sterling, and the annual expenditure on armaments by nearly 28 million.

To provide for this waste, the Income Tax-payers have suffered not a little; but it is the wage-earners who have felt most grievously the sore burdens of increased taxation on sugar, tea, and other necessaries of life. The inevitable results of this squandering of the National wealth have been a lack of employment for the wage-earners, and an attack by the Capitalists on our present fiscal systems of Free Trade. Have nothing to do with 'Fair Trade,' 'Freedom of Negotiation,' 'Retaliation' or 'Preference for the Colonies.' They are all 'Protection' in thin disguise - devices for enriching the Rich at the expense of the Poor. What the Nation requires is not fresh taxes on food and other imports, but a reduction of the present burdens.

In the new Parliament the wrongs done by the late Government will first have to be repaired. In the matter of Education, the management of all Schools supported by the rates and taxes should be entirely under popular control, and no sectarian religion instruction should be permitted therein during school hours. The religious tests which Tory legislation has set up in the selection of persons desiring to qualify as teachers, greater facilities for learning should be provided in unsectarian establishments.

The law relating to Trades Unions must be amended so as to give them freedom and security in the pursuit of their legitimate aims.

I hail with joy the tidings that the Government has arrested the recruiting, embarkation, and importation of Chinese Coolies for labour in the Transvaal mines. They are working there as slaves and bondsmen under degrading conditions, partaking of slavery. Self-government should be granted to the Inhabitants of the Transvaal and Orange River Colonies in the same measure as it is enjoyed by the other Colonies of the Empire. Even the late Tory Ministers acknowledged the principle of government as their guide when they authorised their Lord-Lieutenant to declare, as I do, that 'Ireland should be governed according to Irish ideals.'

Reform of the Land Laws is urgently needed, with the object of bringing back the people to the land, and increasing its productivity.

The laws relating to the incidence of the rates and taxes upon real and personal property require thorough reform, and such reform should include the abolition of the temporary measures passed by the late Parliament which exempts owners of agricultural lands and tithes from a moiety of the rates, to the prejudice of ownership of house property.

The seven years' limit for Parliament to run requires to be curtailed. The Registration of Voters and their exercise of the Franchise should be simplified; and the burden of election expenses removed from the Candidates, so that in this, as in other walks of life, equality of opportunity may be granted to poor and rich alike.

I cannot believe that the existence of the Chamber of Hereditary Legislators will be any longer tolerated if measures passed by a Liberal House of Commons are rejected or mutilated by the House of Lords.

I would add one other word. The wellbeing of the inhabitants of my native Town and Country will always have a place in my heart, and it is to promote their prosperity that I ask for your support, in conjunction with your old and esteemed member Mr Goddard, in this political contest.

I am, Gentlemen,
Your faithful servant,
FELIX COBBOLD
Ipswich, January 1906

As we have seen earlier, Felix did not always follow the party line in full, but here he is in full agreement with Liberal aims. Moreover, he goes further than the more cautious Goddard. Goddard's address supports the abolition of Chinese slavery, land and tax reform, free trade, and reform of the Education Act. Felix has added several more radical aims: the reform of a hereditary House of Lords, the right to belong to Trade Unions, and the right of a Parliamentary candidate to have his expenses paid by the party of the state so that poor men could stand for election. Felix's support for Trade Unions had been in evidence in his speeches before the previous election, in which he supported the right of agricultural workers to combine.

However, while his radical views antagonised his electorate in 1900, now the electorate itself had changed, and non-conformists flocked to the Liberal cause to hasten reform of the Education Act.

Something else had changed: the railway timetable had dominated the electioneering of 1885, and carriages were used extensively in 1900. Now the automobile was being used, which meant that candidates toured their constituencies ceaselessly in their quest for votes. It was an exhausting process for candidates, and must have been particularly trying for a man now in his mid-sixties.

On January 2 the Woodbridge Division Liberal Association held a meeting at the Ipswich Reform Club to adopt R.L. Everett as candidate, with Felix in the chair as President of the Association. The following night there was a large Liberal meeting at the Ipswich Public Hall, complete with a brass band and most of the local candidates. The paper reported that when Felix arrived *"he was received with much cheering and the singing of 'He's a jolly good fellow.'"* Later the meeting sang the Liberal march to the tune of Men of Harlech and an anti-protectionist song, *"Just before the battle, Joseph."* The hall was full to capacity, so it was clearly a successful meeting.

That same night, January 3, a Unionist meeting was held at the Art Gallery in the High Street to adopt Sir Charles Dalrymple and S.G. Hoare as candidates, and Felix was attacked by Hoare as a turncoat, which was duly reported in the press. Referring to religious education he said that *"Mr Cobbold had evidently been to the states recently and visited Utah (laughter). He (the speaker) had never had any intercourse with Mormons, and therefore Mr Cobbold had the advantage of him in that respect. He gathered from Mr Cobbold's remarks that he was not averse to the religious education of the children in the 14,000 non-provided schools in this country being thrown over to the Mormons. (laughter) That seemed to him a very remarkable attitude for a candidate who would have to draw support from a very strict section of the Nonconformist party. (laughter.)"*

The following day Felix's election address, as above, appeared in the paper, and again on January 6. On January 5 he was at a meeting at Springfield Road School, together with Goddard, and the following night they were both at Westerfield and Rushmere. The paper reported that *"Mr Felix Cobbold, who explained that he had already spoken four times that day, delivered a short speech in which he spoke in favour of one man, one vote, also on food taxes and education reform."*

The punishing timetable continued. On the 8th he spoke at Rose Hill Council School at 8.00 pm, and then moved on to Argyle St. Council School. The following day he was at St John National School, and the Memorial Hall at St Clement's. On the 10 he visited Whersted Road Council School, and Bramford Road Council School, and then chaired a meeting of the Governors of East Suffolk and Ipswich Hospital at the Town Hall in Ipswich.

Polling day, 1906

The system of having staggered polling days throughout the country still continued, so Ipswich became the first place in the country to poll on January 12. Lowestoft followed on the 13th, Bury on the 15th, Woodbridge Division on 17th, and Sudbury on 18th. Stevenson was uncontested at Eye so no poll was held, but on January 26 Stowmarket voted.

On the final day of electioneering, January 11, there was another meeting in Ipswich, and a telegram was received from the party leader, Campbell-Bannerman, saying, *"I earnestly call upon Ipswich to set a brilliant example to the whole country tomorrow."* Asquith also wrote saying, *"Good wishes to Cobbold and Goddard. I trust that Ipswich will lead the way to a Free Trade victory."*

Polling day itself provided a final opportunity for the candidates to show their faces to their supporters throughout the constituency. The papers reported that Felix and Goddard appeared together in *"very fine motor cars. Mr Cobbold's was bedecked with yellow and moving very silently. A broad band of yellow round the body of the car and the wheels were covered inside with material of the same colour, producing a very pleasing effect."*

The Crown and Anchor Hotel, as the Liberal headquarters, was almost covered with festoons, rosettes and billows of yellow material, while Dalrymple and Hoare based themselves at the White Horse Hotel.

The results were announced at 12.30pm on the following day at the Town Hall in Ipswich and were a triumph for the Liberals. Goddard had polled 6,396, Felix Cobbold 6,290, while Dalrymple had 4,591 and Hoare 4,232. A screen was erected over the entrance to the Town Hall displaying the results.

The campaigning went on in all the other constituencies, buoyed up with the knowledge that the Ipswich liberal vote had gone so well, and now the Ipswich candidates were free to help their colleagues. On January 15, for example, Felix visited Grundisburgh to support Everett at a meeting, while simultaneously John Dupuis Cobbold and Philip Wyndham Cobbold were at a meeting in Woodbridge supporting Captain Pretyman.

On polling day in Woodbridge Everett drove round the villages of his area in a Gladiator car decked in party colours, accompanied by Felix Cobbold, Mrs Everett and a Mrs Cullingham. The timetable was fierce: they left Felixstowe at 8.30 am, arriving at Trimley at 8.50, Bucklesham at 9.10, and Otley at 12.45. Lunch had been at 1.45 pm. Then it was on to the Swan Hotel, Needham Market at 2.30. They reached Claydon at 4.05, Shotley at 7.10pm, and back to Ipswich at 8.00 pm, having visited 28 places in all. At the same time Captain Pretyman went on his own twelve-hour motor journey. Leaving Orwell Park house at 8.00 am, he also visited Bucklesham and Trimley, and perhaps passed Everett and Cobbold on the way. He was accompanied by Lady Beatrice Pretyman and a Mr B. Norman. They took lunch at Wickham Market and finally arrived back in Ipswich at 7.45 pm having visited 30 places. His efforts were in vain: on polling day Everett took the seat by 5,527 votes to 5,348.

All over the country the same effect was seen: nonconformists everywhere rallied to the Liberal cause, hoping for reformation of the Education Act, together with supporters of free trade. The final results for the Parliament were that the Liberals had 386 seats, and could call on support from the 41 Labour seats, and 84 Nationalists, while the Unionists had only 156 seats.

1906 Parliament

On February 15 Parliament opened with Campbell-Bannerman as Prime Minister, and Felix was back in Westminster after twenty-one years. One obituary in the East Anglian Daily Times of 1909 gives us glimpses of his life as an MP:

"Mr Cobbold was assiduous in his attention to duty, though he did not often seek to catch the Speaker's eye, and was well content with a seat on the back benches. One distinctive feature of his Parliamentary career was his warm support of a peace policy..... He was among the foremost of those who strongly condemned what he believed to be excessive armaments, and more than once tabled amendments to Navy Estimates, and acted as Teller in Divisions. Mr Cobbold, moreover, had warm sympathy and appreciation for the work and ideals of the Labour groups, amongst whom he occasionally sat in the House of Commons, although his usual place was under the gallery.

We believe, indeed, that the last speech Mr Cobbold made in Ipswich was in the Public Hall on the 6 September 1908 when he assisted in offering a welcome to the delegates to the Trade Union Congress." This is significant when we recall his support for trade unionism in both 1900 and 1906.

Felix rarely spoke in the house, but he was an acknowledged expert on finance, and used this skill in committees. As a member of the Armaments Committee in June 1906 he complained bitterly about the excessive number of troops stationed in Malta. Indeed there were so many that an extra charge of £600 had to be allocated for hire of buildings to supplement the overcrowded barracks. The chairman asked him to confine himself to the vote, but Felix persisted by complaining that the harbour was already a cesspool of drainage, in consequence of the number of troops and ships of war quartered there. He had clearly researched this well, as he now produced figures from the Army Medical Report which compared Malta, Gibraltar, Egypt and Cyprus.

"In 1903 those constantly ineffective from sickness at Malta numbered 45.34 per 1000, whilst at Gibraltar the figures were 29.87, and in Egypt and Cyprus only 44.49."

It was clear that Felix shunned the centre stage, but worked tirelessly on committees not only in Westminster but also in Ipswich and Felixstowe although he was in increasingly poor health. The Yorkshire Herald commented after his death that... *"Mr Cobbold was a quiet, retiring gentleman. His modest demeanour and gentle manner was, however, the outward cloth of an extreme Radical. This Radicalism surprised both political friends and enemies."*

Eventually the overwork took its toll. In November 1909 he spent a short and happy holiday at his Felixstowe home and farm, but caught a chill. He returned to London, intending to return home again the following weekend. He never reached the House of Commons: his health worsened with an acute "kidney disorder," and a Dr. Coleman and Mr Sargant, both from St Thomas' Hospital, were called, together with Sir Victor Horseley. They decided to operate, and he then returned to his rooms in Whitehall Court to recuperate, nursed almost alone by his sister, Constance Green. For a week and a half he seemed to be recovering, but then suddenly deteriorated, and died early on Monday morning, December 6 1909.

Felix had asked that his body should be cremated as soon as possible, and this took place at Golders Green crematorium on 8 December. However, if he had planned to disappear with little fuss, his family and friends thought otherwise. At the same time a Memorial Service was held at St Mary-le-Tower, Ipswich, and the following day a second service was held at St Margaret's Church, Westminster, *'for the convenience of the gentleman's London friends.'*

The newspapers reported the two events in detail: every important guest was named, and the music played by the honorary organist, the Conservative Mr Bunnell Burton, was named, including *"The Lost Chord."* The bells were muffled, all but the great bell which had been given to the church by John Chevallier Cobbold, and this was left 'open' by the request of the family. The mayor wore his full regalia and assembled with the Town Council at the Town Hall. The group then processed to the church headed by the sword and mace bearers who carried the regalia draped in black, while the Mayor's chain was also draped in black.

Representatives from all the organisations associated with Felix, often in the role of chairman or President or vice-president, attended, so the church was packed. These included The Ipswich Male Voice Choir, of which Felix was a vice-president, the Ipswich Early Closing Association, the Ipswich Municipal Secondary Schools, of which Felix was a Governor, the Ipswich Teachers' Musical and Dramatic Society. There were also, of course, representatives from the Hospital, the Bank - now renamed Capital & Counties Bank - and all the Liberal Associations from the area.

The London service attracted a smaller congregation, but was still called 'impressive' by the East Anglian Daily Times. A large group of family members travelled down to be present, along with Lord Gwydyr, Lord Coleridge, Lord Lochee, Lord & Lady Cairns, and a large group of MPs. For a quiet and modest man it was an imposing farewell.

For most mortals, a funeral would mark the end of their life's work, but this was the end of the life of Felix Thornley Cobbold, a man who had been planning his legacy for years, and had determined to leave his mark on his town and his county. The results of much of his planning were still to be seen.

Chapter 8 - Felix's legacy - the plan revealed

Gippeswyk Park

For a week the papers had been giving reports of the death of Felix Cobbold and the two services. However, on the 14 December it was revealed by The Times, The Eastern Daily Press and the East Anglian that at the time of his death Felix had been planning another gift to Ipswich, that of Gippeswyk Park.

Philip Wyndham Cobbold, the executor of Felix's estate, wrote to the Mayor to reveal that Felix had been in the process of transferring to the Corporation some 45 acres of land of the Gippeswyk Park estate, beside the Great Eastern Railway Line. The gift was to have been transferred on December 6, which was the day of Felix's death, but Philip decided that the transaction would still take place as soon as the legal processes would allow, and had written the letter to the Mayor on the 11th so that his uncle's wishes might be carried out precisely.

The East Anglian devoted several columns to the purchase, revealing that it had been an old plan of Felix's. The land had been bought by the third Lord Gwydyr in 1851, but he had not been willing to sell the land to Felix. Later Felix approached the fourth Lord Gwydyr, but the 1906 election was called shortly and Felix thought it imprudent to make such a gift before the election as it would have seemed like a bribe to the town. However, when the fourth Lord died in April 1909 Felix approached his heir, and the purchase was finally agreed.

Felix planned that the land should be surrounded by an iron railing at his expense, and this was now to be erected by Philip Cobbold. Lord Gwydyr had widened Gippeswyk Avenue to 45 ft. to improve access, while preserving the line of trees along the Avenue. The Corporation already owned one field abutting the Avenue and Wallers Grove, and access to the new public park could be arranged through this Corporation land. The parkland had been used in recent years by various athletic clubs and the Ipswich and District Football League and its junior branch, and Felix intended that it should continue to be used in this way as playing fields.[1]

---

[1] Visitors to the area today may note that on passing the area of the park they travel down to the town past the current Ipswich Town Football Stadium with its prominent Cobbold stand, highlighting the continued commitment of the family to supporting Ipswich sports facilities.

The Ipswich Evening Star commented on 21 December that with a large town... *"spreading its tentacles regardless of beauty spots and the convenience of those locked in their interiors, it is good to have a few spots kept holy from the intruding grasp of the builder, and future generations will have reason to bless the man who ensured the town a breathing place amidst a wilderness of bricks and mortar."*

Christchurch Mansion

Philip Cobbold's letter to the Mayor on 11 December revealed a further gift to the town. Felix had wanted to augment his gift to the town of Christchurch Mansion by providing funds *"for the purchase and housing of works and objects of art."* The Museum Committee running the Mansion had always been crippled by lack of funds, but Felix had now given them £20,000 sterling Ipswich Corporation Three-percent stock, so that the annual interest of around £600 could be used for purchases. Previously the Committee had had available for the stocking and maintenance of the Mansion the product of a penny-halfpenny rate, which in 1908 produced £1,010 10s, some of which went to pay off previous debts and which left only a small sum available for maintenance. The Council had been giving an annual grant of £150, but nevertheless the accounts showed a total deficit of £45 3s. 10d. at the end of 1908. One can imagine their relief at the news of the permanent help given them by Felix's carefully arranged gift.

The family

Although these two gifts were revealed by Philip Cobbold on 11 December, it was not until February 8 1910 that the rest of the will was revealed after probate, and a copy is included in an Appendix on page 79.

It is in itself a work of art. I have surmised earlier in chapter 4 that Felix probably began planning it in 1886 after the death of his brothers, although the final version was only signed on 11 September, 1908. The will reveals that he had been quietly buying up agricultural land for his primary interest of improving the lot of agricultural workers, and indeed his work as a banker meant that he had been in a privileged position of finding out what was coming up for sale and negotiating with the previous owners. The next chapter will examine this part of the bequests in detail.

The total estate gross value amounted to £407,790 15s. 9d, and the sole executor was Philip Wyndham Cobbold of Kesgrave Hall. Apart from the agricultural items, the bequests are mostly to members of his family. What is remarkable is that fourteen of these gifts were to women - his sisters, and his nieces. For example, to his niece Isabel Amy Chevallier, wife of John Barrington Trapnell Chevallier, he gave £5,000. The nephews were not excluded, but the emphasis on the gifts to women is unusual for its time. Felix himself said *"those (gifts) given to married women shall be for their sole and separate use, free and independent of their husbands...."* It is a thoughtful detail in the will, revealing perhaps another aspect to Felix's radical views: support for the rights of women and the property of married women in particular.

King's College Chapel

The next significant section of the will concerns King's College, Cambridge. As bursar he had supervised repairs to the buildings and certain additions, and he now gave them a sum of £10,000, *"to be used at their sole discretion in any addition they may make to their Collegiate buildings, and so far as the money hereby bequeathed may not be so applied, then I direct that they hold the part unapplied as a Chapel Fund, and apply the interest from any securities upon which the same may be invested, towards the maintenance and repair of the fabric of the Chapel or of the internal fittings, including the glazed windows."*

Here again, the evidence of careful thought in the framing of this will is shown: he did not want to tie the hands of the College if they needed funds for other projects, but above all he wanted some of his money to be used for the maintenance of the magnificent chapel that he had clearly enjoyed so much during his years in Cambridge.

The Bank

By this time the various Cobbold banking interests had been merged under the name of Capital & Counties Bank, which was then acquired by Lloyds Bank. However, in his will Felix had given his nephew, Herbert St George all the interest of banking accounts kept under the name of the old Bacon, Cobbold & Co. Bank in Ipswich and elsewhere, and a second nephew, Herbert Jervis White Jervis, similarly inherited interest in accounts for the Harwich bank, Cox, Cobbold & Co. His estate was to bear the cost of any estate or death duties on the value of these banking accounts and securities, and would also pay *"any loss occasioned in the ultimate winding up of the said late Banking firm's assets."*

Felix had remained a senior partner of the banks to the time of his death, and he had reason to be grateful for the privileges these businesses gave him: not only considerable wealth, but also an insight into the growth of the area, personal contacts, and the opportunity to purchase property whenever it came up for sale.

It gave him something else: the mind of a banker. Throughout his life his financial skills had grown, first through his work as a bursar, and then by the many years he spent working as a banker at a time when the work was 'hands on' and more of an art form than it is today. Face to face interviews with his clients and the making of fine judgements filled his days, and the complexities of this final document reveal his mature skills in financial management.

Felix the Philanthropist

Towards the end of his Mayoral year Felix spoke about his views on the proper use of wealth, and these were mentioned in an obituary from the East Anglian Daily Times on December 6 1909. *"A great deal,"* he remarked, *"had been said about his generosity, but when he heard that, he was always reminded of the sayings of two people - one was Becky Sharp, the heroine of 'Vanity Fair' who, though not particularly virtuous herself, always, when she looked at others who were so, said it was 'easy to be virtuous on £5,000 a year.' The other was Mr Carnegie, who said, 'the man who died rich died dishonoured.' That was too hard a saying for him, but he took Becky Sharp and Mr Carnegie, and tried to find a medium between the two."*

He had indeed achieved the balance he had sought by distributing wealth, not only during his lifetime - the many small gifts to those who needed help and the major gifts to Ipswich - but also after his death. The carefully planned distribution of his remaining wealth meant that his money would go on working for his major life concerns - Ipswich and agriculture - far into the future.

Chapter 9 - The Felix Cobbold Agricultural Trust

Agriculture in the nineteenth century

To understand the significance of the legacy of Felix Cobbold to the agricultural scene it is necessary to look again at the background problems, which I referred to briefly in Chapter 2.

Agriculture had been in a state of depression since 1873. At first it had looked like a brief period of bad luck which would be balanced by a future run of better fortune. It began mainly with a spell of bad weather: a wet autumn of 1875 was followed by heavy rain in the winter of 1876-7, and then from early 1878 began a period of two and a half years of exceptional cold and heavy rainfall. Heavy snow led to severe floods in 1878, and the following winter was long and severe. And so it went on until 1882, and the brief lull in 1883 was followed by a drought the following years.

In the heavy clay lands of East Anglia the wet years were disastrous: fields lay waterlogged and unworkable, and the areas left as fallow rose by a third. The wet had other effects: there was an epidemic of liver rot in sheep in 1878-82, and severe foot-and-mouth in 1881-3. Sheep numbers fell throughout the period in East Anglia, although landowners worked hard to develop better breeds and the Suffolk Sheep Breed Society was formed in 1885

Cattle were similarly hit: between 1853 and 1874 there were attacks of rinderpest, pleuro-pneumonia and foot-and-mouth disease. This produced a similar interest in developing stock resistant to disease, and the Suffolk Red Poll herd-books date from 1874.

The third problem was that of foreign imported food. The railways in East Anglia helped farmers to distribute their produce to towns like London, but railways also helped American farmers to open up the vast areas of fertile virgin land on the prairies. Thus at a time when British farmers were being struck by bad weather, there was a flood of American wheat and barley, so that prices fell disastrously. An acre of wheat in Rendlesham in 1874 could raise £8 13s 1s, but in 1894 this had fallen to £3 12s 6d. This meant slow ruin for hundreds of small farmers, and they asked for the return of the Corn Laws. By contrast, townspeople campaigned for free trade and cheap food.

By 1885, meat sales were also threatened: food refrigeration techniques were developed and this meant that frozen meat could be imported. By 1895 over a third of British consumption came from abroad, but it was poorer in quality than British meat, so the home market held its own despite the competition.

However, most farms in Suffolk were arable rather than livestock, and their slow decline continued unabated. Bailiffs began to complain that tenants were leaving their farms and it was impossible to find new tenants. Rents fell, but still the number of untended farms increased. In 1882 a member of the Royal Commission investigating the farming situation reported, *"I was told on good authority that one might drive almost from Newmarket to Brandon, a distance of 15 or 16 miles, without passing land in occupation of a tenant."*

Fewer farmers also meant fewer farm workers. Labourers, already the victims of poor housing and low wages, flooded into towns looking for work, taking with them their agricultural skills, or sought immigration.

The Felix Cobbold bequest

Against this background, politicians like Jesse Collings and Joseph Chamberlain developed their schemes for creating smallholdings whereby labourers could work the land for themselves, and perhaps diversify into other cash crops like fruit. Felix Cobbold had seen the misery of farmers every week at the Bank, and became an enthusiastic proponent of these ideas and began buying up farmland, and offering plots at a small annual rent. In his will, however, he went further: he donated over 850 acres of land in Hadleigh, Hintlesham and Sproughton to East Suffolk County Council. He also donated all the crops at present growing on the land, together with the carts and farm implements, and a sum of money. The entire bequest came with a request that it was to be kept by the Council on trust to develop small holdings and allotments. If the Council refused the bequest, the land would revert to his residuary and personal estate.

These terms posed a problem for the Council for by the Mortmain Act of 1888 the Council was not able to acquire land even for a charitable purpose without a special licence. Secondly, by the Smallholdings and Allotment Act of 1908, the Council was empowered to acquire land for the purpose of providing smallholdings and allotments, but allotments were actually to be provided by Urban or Parish Councils. One property, known as Arnold's Field in Hadleigh, actually lay outside their area and posed a separate problem. Finally, if the problems of Mortmain and the administration of the allotments could be overcome, the rents derived had to be kept in a separate fund and administered as a trust.

However, by 1910 the difficulties were surmounted. The Charity Commissioners made an order in March that the land could be administered as a charity under the title of 'Felix T. Cobbold's Smallholdings and Allotments Trust.' Further clauses stipulated that allotments should not exceed one acre, and that smallholdings were to be between one and fifty acres, unless at the time of letting the value for the purposes of income tax did not exceed £50. The intentions of the bequest were further protected in that holdings were not to be used for any other purpose than agriculture, and that the holdings should be cultivated by the tenant, not more than one dwelling-house should be erected on each holding, and these must comply with the Trustees' requirements which secured *"healthiness and freedom from overcrowding,"* and that *"no dwelling-house or buildings shall be used for the sale of intoxicating liquors."*

The scheme worked well, providing just such employment as Felix had envisaged for local poor agricultural workers, and between the wars additional land was bought by the Trust at Great Blakenham and Witnesham.

However, by the 1960s agricultural conditions had altered so much that the Trust felt that the original aims were no longer valid and changes were needed. Therefore, on 31 May 1966, a new Trust Deed was adopted which stated that:

"The object of the Charity shall be by establishing and maintaining a farm or farms as centres for demonstrating, training, and apprenticing and by other means to advance and improve agriculture, and, in particular, to educate farmers and young persons in agricultural methods, development and techniques."

Part of the original land at Sproughton was retained to provide funds, but the rest was gradually sold so that a compact estate suitable for the new enterprises could be purchased. The Sproughton estate eventually comprised 70.003 acres, (including a plantation of 3.21 acres of sycamore and Scots pine), and comprised Hope Farm and 2.249 acres of allotments which were let to Sproughton Parish Council.

Demonstration Farm

The Trust bought Stanaway and Charity Farms at Otley for the purposes of establishing a Demonstration Farm - an area of 376.405 acres, and in 1991 an additional 182 acres were purchased at Ashbocking. The purpose of the land was agreed by the Trustees as:

"...managing a commercially profitable farm with average working conditions, providing facilities for the College students (see below) *and staging those demonstrations that one could manage under these conditions."*

This work continued until 2006.

Otley College

In order to fulfil the object of *"educating farmers and young persons"*, the Trust approached East Suffolk Agricultural Education Centre with an exciting proposition for support and co-operation. Despite the grand name, the Centre had been started by Graham Boatfield and Brian Bell as a two-room building, with fifty students and *"a few bits and pieces of machinery."* The enterprise had grown through local demand until it had three lecture rooms and workshops, and two hundred day students. However, as demand continued to grow East Suffolk Education Committee decided that better premises had to be provided.

Here the Trust found an ideal partner for its work, and in 1970 a range of buildings and an area of 5.627 acres were provided on the Felix Cobbold Trust land at Otley, at a cost of £80,000, on a ninety-nine year lease. The Centre moved in under the new name of East Suffolk Agricultural Institute, later Otley College of Agriculture and Horticulture, and in 1994 changed again to Otley College, reflecting the wider interests of the developing college.

The Trust continued to be a benevolent patron of the College and not merely a landlord. Over the years the lease was amended several times so that an increased acreage was granted to the College, until by 1992 a total of 40.44 acres was leased until the year 2068. Some of the original buildings, which had been retained as part of the Demonstration Farm stores, became living accommodation for students and Stanaway Farmhouse was occupied by the Farm Foreman of the Demonstration Farm.

The Trust helped in other ways: in 1994, for example, it donated money for the computerisation of the growing library, and since 1973 grants have been made for Study Visits for students visiting European agricultural organisations - a programme that grew with the establishment of the European Union. Thus by 1994 the Trust was contributing £15,000 to the visits programme.

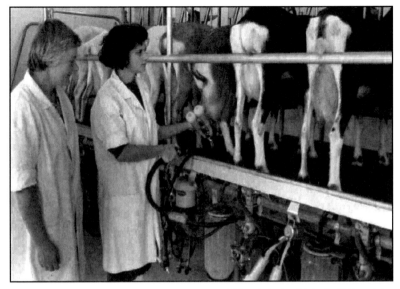

Otley student and tutor in College dairy

Trust reorganisation from 2006

The agricultural situation has continued to change, which meant that from 2006 the Trust decided once again to reorganise. The work of the Demonstration Farm has come to an end, and the running costs and staff expenses can now be diverted to other uses, and, in addition, the farm machinery and some parcels of land have been sold. Stanaway and Hope Farmhouses have been let for residential use, and three other buildings at Stanaway were let to commercial tenants.

The overall effect is that revenue has been increased considerably, and all rents from the properties and allotments etc. can be diverted to charitable purposes. The new Deed states that:

"The Trust's overall objective is to advance and improve agriculture, and in particular, to educate and inform farmers and young persons in agricultural methods, developments and techniques."

77

Grants are now given for:
1) Education and Training
2) Research and Development
3) Promotion and publicity
4) Capital and equipment
5) Production and marketing
6) Environmental activities and wildlife.

Projects being supported are now not just in Suffolk, although applicants *"must be living or originate from Suffolk and adjoining counties"*, an area wider than the original boundaries of the old East Suffolk County Council, reflecting the growing regionalisation of agriculture.

Felix Cobbold himself would have no doubt approved of the continuing work of the Trust. Here is a lasting benefit from his money, as thousands of students leave training and apprenticeships to enter the land-based industries, pursue experimental research projects for higher degrees, and battle with climate change and new pests and diseases. The demands and challenges for farmers and their employees have changed in a way that Felix could not have foreseen but the Trust has adapted and will, no doubt, continue to change. Felix's foresight and determination to improve the lot of land workers has been fully vindicated, and East Anglian agriculture has continued to benefit from his gifts. (see www.felixcobboldtrust.org.uk)

Appendix - Felix Thornley Cobbold's will

Probate for this will was granted on February 5th 1910. The gross amount of the estate was £407,790 15s. 9d. and the net personalty was £322,456 14s 8d.

"I bequeath to my sister, Lucy Jervis White Jervis, a sum of £10,000; to my sister, Constance Sophia Green, a sum of £10,000; to my niece, Aline Hope, wife of George Palmer Hope, of the London Stock Exchange, a sum of £2,000; to my nephew, Sir John Jervis White Jervis, a sum of £10,000; to my niece, Edith Julia Monins, wife of John Henry Monins, of Ringwood, Kent, a sum of £15,000; to my niece, Adela Lucy Ricardo, wife of Henry George Ricardo, a retired Major in the Royal Artillery, a sum of £15,000; to my niece, Olive Cairns, wife of Wilfrid Earl Cairns, a sum of £10,000; to my niece, Evelyn Anna Cobbold, a sum of £10,000; to my nephew, Christian Chevallier Cobbold, a sum of £5,000; to my niece, Maud Chevallier Anderson, wife of Charles Anderson, M.D., a sum of £2,000; to my niece, Laura Cobbold, daughter of my late brother, Ernest St George Cobbold, a sum of £1,000; to my niece, Helen Mary Cobbold, a sum of £5,000; to my niece, Isabel Amy Chevallier, wife of John Barrington Trapnell Chevallier, a sum of £5,000; to my niece, Elsie M Cobbold, a sum of £1,000; to my niece, Sibyl C Porter, wife of Gerald Lachlan Porter, a sum of £1,000; to my niece, Violet A Riley, wife of Rupert Riley, a sum of £1,000; to my nephew, Ernest Cazenova Cobbold, a Major in the Army, a sum of £1,000; to my nephew Herbert St George Cobbold, a sum of £35,000; to my nephew, Clement John Fromanteel Cobbold, a sum of £30,000; to my cousin, Charles Herbert Cobbold, of Needlewood, Barnsley, Yorkshire, a sum of £1,000; And I direct that all the above legacies shall be paid free of legacy duty and of estate duty, and all other death duties, and that those given to married women shall be for their sole and separate use, free and independent of their husbands, and I direct that interest shall run on all such legacies at £4 per centum per annum from the date of my death until they are paid, and the payment of such interest to be made half-yearly, and the first payment to be made at the expiration of six months from my death.

I bequeath to my nephew, Ralph Patteson Cobbold,, a retired Major in the Army, a sum of £10,000; to the Provost and Scholars of King's College, Cambridge, a sum of £10,000 to be used at their sole discretion in any addition they may make to their Collegiate buildings, and so far as the money hereby bequeathed may not be so applied, then I direct that they hold the part unapplied as a Chapel Fund, and apply the interest from any securities upon which the same may be invested, towards the maintenance and repair of the fabric of the Chapel or of the internal fittings, including the glazed windows.

I bequeath to the Mayor and Burgesses of the Borough of Ipswich a sum of £20,000 Ipswich Corporation Stock, now standing in my name, in case I shall not have transferred the said amount of stock to them in my lifetime, in which case this bequest becomes inoperative, and I direct that they hold the said sum of £20,000 Ipswich Stock, or the securities from time to time representing the same, in trust to apply the dividends from time to time as they think fit, with full power to accumulate the same in the purchase of objects of art, pictures, statues, furniture, prints, drawings, or any other works of art, to be placed in Christchurch Mansion in Ipswich, which I presented to the Borough some years ago; and I direct they may apply as much as one-sixth of the yearly income or accumulations, in fittings in and about the Mansion, suitable for the reception of such works of art, and in the repairs of the Mansion itself.

I direct that the said legacy to my nephew, Ralph Patteson Cobbold, and also the legacy to the Provost and Fellows of King's College, Cambridge, and also the specific legacy to the Mayor and Burgesses of Ipswich, be paid and transferred to them free of legacy and estate duties and all other death duties.

I give to my nephew, Herbert St George Cobbold, all the interest I have in any banking account kept under the names of the late firm of Bacon, Cobbold and Co. at Ipswich and elsewhere, and to my nephew, Herbert Jervis White Jervis, all the interest I have in any banking accounts kept under the name of the late firm of Cox, Cobbold & Co. at Harwich; and all the interest which belongs to me in the unliquidated securities and properties of such late banking firms to be included in such respective gifts. And I direct my executor, to pay the ascertained legacy and estate and other death duties on the value of such banking accounts and securities, and any loss occasioned in the ultimate winding up of the said late Banking firm's assets.

I devise and bequeath my real estate, at Hadleigh and Hintlesham, called Pond Hall Farm, and the Valley Farm, and the Ramsey Farm, and also my land at Sproughton, which is occupied in small holdings and allotments, and as respects the Hadleigh and Hintlesham farms, all the growing crops and stock on the farms, live and dead, and all the carts and other farming implements, and the banking account kept at the Ipswich Capital & Counties Bank, under the name of George T. Harrison, Pond Hall Account, to the East Suffolk County Council, upon trust that they use the said hereditaments and personal estate, and the rents and profits arising therefrom in developing small holdings and allotments on so much of the land in Hadleigh as is not already so occupied, and on any other land that they may acquire by means of such rents and profits. And in case the East Suffolk Council refuse to accept the above devise and bequest, or are disqualified by law from accepting the same, then I direct that the said hereditaments at Hadleigh and Hintlesham and Sproughton, and the said farming stock and money at the said banking account shall fall into and form part of my residuary real and personal estate.

I bequeath to my friend, George T. Harrison, of Holton St Mary, Suffolk, a sum of £500, free of legacy and estate and all other death duties, such sum of £500 to be paid out of my general residuary estate, and not out of the estate above specifically devised and bequeathed.

All the rest and residue of my real and personal estate whatever at Felixstowe, Ipswich, Little Blakenham, Eye, and Rattlesden, in Suffolk or elsewhere, all my moneys and securities for money, furniture, books, horses, carriages, wines, stores, goods and effects, I give and devise and bequeath to my nephew, Philip Wyndham Cobbold, his heirs and assigns absolutely, and I appoint him sole executor and trustee of this my will.

Felix further decreed that this body should be cremated with all possible speed after this death.

Bibliography

Cobbold, Felix T.: *Balance Sheets and Private Memoranda Book*
(in the possession of Lloyds Bank Archives), 1886-1893
Cobbold, Felix T: Two letters to Henry Bradshaw (in the possession of
King's College Modern Archive Collection, Cambridge)
Ernle, Lord: *English Farming Past and Present*, 6th edition, London, Heinemann, 1961
Felixstowe Board: *Guide to Felixstowe*, 1893
Jacobson, Michael: *The Cliff Brewery 1723-1973*, Ipswich, Tollemache and Cobbold 1973
James M.R.: *Eton and Kings. Recollections, mostly trivial 1875-1925*,
Williams & Norgate, London, 1926
Kelly's Directory of Ipswich, Kelly and Co, London, 1906
Jarrold's Directory of Ipswich, Norwich, 1890
Lee, S.J.: *Aspects of British Political History, 1815-1914*. Routledge, 1994
Maltby, R.: *Felixstowe, a pictorial history*, Chichester, Phillimore Press, 1992
Murphy D, Staton R, Walsh-Atkins P, Whiskerd N: *Britain 1783-1918*,
London, Collins Educational, 2003
Orwin & Whetham: *History of British Agriculture 1846-1914*
Oxford Dictionary of National Biography (online version)
The Parliamentary Debates, (4th series) Vol 1 (Feb 1892) to Vol 199 (Dec 1908)
Royal Commission on Agriculture, 1879-1882 *Mr Druce's Report: Suffolk*
Chaired by the Duke of Richmond, Great Britain
Royal Commission on Agriculture *Report*, Great Britain, 1895, Appendix A
Seaver, George, *Autobiography* (unpublished)
Stevens Directory of Ipswich, G. Stevens, London, 1885
"*Suffolk County Handbook and Official Directory*", 1909
White: *History, Gazeteer and Directory of Suffolk*, Sheffield, 1889, 1900
Wikipedia online encyclopedia
Withers, John J.: *A Register of Admissions to King's College, Cambridge 1797-1925*,
London, John Murray 1929

Contemporary newspaper reports from:

East Anglian Daily Times
Ipswich Chronicle
Ipswich Journal
Ipswich Observer and Felixstowe Times
Suffolk Chronicle

Obituaries of Felix Cobbold taken from various National newspapers mounted in a scrapbook
in the possession of the Cobbold Family Trust.

THE COBBOLD FAMILY HISTORY TRUST

The COBBOLD FAMILY HISTORY TRUST has three main purposes - Firstly, to collect and preserve, safely and permanently, family memorabilia: books, pictures, photographs, papers and artefacts. It was started to accept the settlor's own collection, but has since grown by deposit and gift. Depositors have often expressed relief and satisfaction that lifelong and treasured possessions have found a safe home. The Trust is non-aggressive; it does not seek items with which the owner does not wish to part, but it actively seeks items that would otherwise be lost, destroyed or fragmented.

Secondly, the Trust wishes to grow the family tree to the point where it can be beneficially published. Thirdly, and resulting mainly from the first two objectives, the Trust provides a substantial resource for family members and family historians in this and future generations.

In this fast changing world of expendability, obsolescence and disposability the remarkable and historically important family possessions of the past will vanish unless we bring them together and make them safe now. To achieve this the Trust relies solely on donations and deposits from friends and family members.

For further information on the work of the Trust, see the website at **www.cobboldfht.com**

As building a family history is inevitably a step-by-step process, readers who feel they have a contribution to make are positively encouraged to contact the Cobbold Family History Trust at:

14, Moorfields, Moorhaven, Ivybridge, Devon PL21 0XQ, United Kingdom

Index

(Page numbers in italics indicate illustrations)